THE NEW OXFORD PICTURE DICTIONARY

Beginner's Workbook

by

PATRICIA E. ZEVIN

Oxford University Press

Oxford University Press

198 Madison Avenue
New York, NY 10016 USA

Great Clarendon Street
Oxford OX2 6DP England

Oxford New York
Athens Auckland Bangkok Bogota Buenos Aires Calcutta Cape Town
Chennai Dar es Salaam Delhi Florence Hong Kong Istanbul Karachi
Kuala Lumpur Madrid Melbourne Mexico City Mumbai Nairobi Paris
Sao Paulo Singapore Taipei Tokyo Toronto Warsaw

OXFORD is a trademark of Oxford University Press.

ISBN 0-19-434326-X

Senior Editor: Margot Gramer
Associate Editor: Mary Lynne Nielsen
Designer: April Okano

Illustrations by Laura Hartman and Raymond Skibinski

Printing (last digit): 20 19 18 17 16 15 14 13

Printed in the United States of America.

To my husband, Gene, who helped me find a room of my own.

Contents

*These lessons include exercises recycling previous vocabulary.

Acknowledgments

I want to express my gratitude to all those colleagues and students with whom I have worked over the years. I have learned from all of you.

Special thanks go to Margot Gramer and Mary Lynne Nielsen, my editors at Oxford University Press, for their patient and knowledgeable assistance. In addition, I want to thank Janet Hafner, James Harlow, Miriam Jupp, Arlene Lighthall, James Middleton, Olga Mirasav, and Libier Woods for their help and interest.

I appreciate, more than I can say, the contributions of Katheryn Garlow and Yvonne Kieran, who started me on this project in the beginning and who continue to be there when I need them. The best part of writing the *Beginner's Workbook* has been talking it over with these good friends and fine teachers.

To the Teacher

The *Beginner's Workbook* for *The New Oxford Picture Dictionary* is designed to provide the learner of English with systematic and enjoyable vocabulary practice.

The *Beginner's Workbook* is intended for use with *The New Oxford Picture Dictionary*, and vocabulary is generally presented in the same order as in the Dictionary.*

The *Beginner's Workbook* divides logically into two semesters' work, with Lessons 1–38 in the first semester and Lessons 39–76 in the second. Each lesson in the *Beginner's Workbook* focuses on specific Dictionary pages. The format is such, however, that each lesson is independently organized, and teachers may make choices to fit any class schedule.

Every effort is made to afford the entry-level student a successful learning experience in group or independent study, beginning with simplified instructions and abundant examples. Any instructions in green ink indicate that vocabulary from an earlier lesson is reviewed in that exercise. Sample answers are also shown in green.

Teachers will note that the varied exercises and the wording of instructions throughout the *Beginner's Workbook* are structured to help the student acquire those basic learning skills needed for further study.

* Lessons on prepositions are presented twice in the *Beginner's Workbook* (Lessons 18 and 35; Lessons 76 and 77).

THE NEW OXFORD PICTURE DICTIONARY

Beginner's Workbook

A. What's the Answer?

▶ Look at the pictures in the Dictionary.
▶ Fill in the blanks.
▶ Write the sentence.

sister	wife	daughter
mother	father	son

1. Mary and Bob Smith are husband and w _i_ _f_ _e_ .

Mary and Bob Smith are husband and wife.

2. Tim Smith is their s ___ ___ .

_____

3. Sally Ann Smith is their d ___ ___ ___ ___ ___ ___ ___ .

_____

4. Sally Ann Smith is Tim Smith's s ___ ___ ___ ___ ___ .

_____

5. Tom Jones is Mary Smith's f ___ ___ ___ ___ ___ .

_____

6. Elizabeth Jones is Mary Smith's m ___ ___ ___ ___ ___ .

_____

1

B. What's Missing?

▶ Fill in the blank.

▶ Write the word.

1. m _a_ n   _man_   **5.** p ___ r e n t s   _____

2. w ___ m a n   _____   **6.** c h ___ l d r e n   _____

3. w ___ f e   _____   **7.** g ___ r l   _____

4. h ___ s b a n d   _____   **8.** b ___ y   _____

C. Who's Who?

▶ Fill in the blanks.

1. grandfather   grandmother

2. father   _mother_____

3. _____   wife

4. _____   daughter

5. brother   _____

6. brother-in-law   _____

7. _____   aunt

8. _____   niece

9. grandson   _____

10. father-in-law   _____

2

D. What Do You Say?

► Fill in the blanks with the names of your relatives.

My Family   **Name**

1. Mother: _____

2. Father: _____

3. Husband/Wife: _____

4. Children: _____

5. Brothers: _____

6. Sisters: _____

7. Grandfathers: _____

8. Grandmothers: _____

9. Aunts: _____

10. Uncles: _____

11. Cousins: _____

E. First and Last

► Circle the first name.
► Underline the last name.

1. (Sally) Ann Smith   **3.** Joseph Bates

2. Peg Carter   **4.** Virginia Bates

5. What's your first name? _____

6. What's your last name? _____

2 The Human Body pages 4–5

A. What Do You See?

▶ Look at the picture.
▶ Write the words.

knee	hair	hand	ankle
chest	arm	elbow	throat

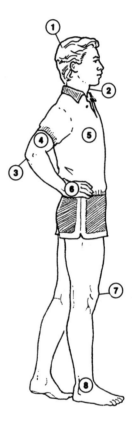

1. __hair_____

2. _____

3. _____

4. _____

5. _____

6. _____

7. _____

8. _____

B. What's Different?

▶ Fill in the blanks.
▶ Circle the word ending in a different letter.

1. l i ___   h i ___   c h i ___

2. n e c ___   b a c ___   c h e s ___

4

C. What Goes Together?

► Write words for the part of the body.

Head

1. _hair_

2. _____

3. _____

Face

1. _____

2. _____

3. _____

Eye

1. _____

2. _____

3. _____

Hand

1. _____

2. _____

3. _____

Leg

1. _____

2. _____

3. _____

Foot

1. _____

2. _____

3. _____

D. You're the Artist

► Draw a face and label all the parts.

► Write the words on the picture.

E. First and Last

► Circle the correct letter.

1. The **first** letter of each word:

(n)eck   throat   chest   back

2. The **last** letter of each word:

wais(t)   mouth   wrist   tooth

3. The **first two** letters of each word:

(ch)eek   chin   chest   brain

4. The words beginning with **w**:

(waist)   wrist   mouth   tooth

5. The words ending in **th**:

waist   wrist   (mouth)   tooth

F. My Driver's License

► Fill in the blanks.

STATE DRIVER'S LICENSE

Name _____
        (first)   (middle)   (last)

Sex ☐ ☐ Color of Hair _____ Color of Eyes _____
     male female

Height _____ Weight _____ Date of Birth _____
                                              day   month   year

Expires on Birthday   1990

3 Vegetables pages 6–7

A. What Is It?

► Look at the picture.
► Write the word.

carrots	lettuce	pepper	tomato	corn
peas	celery	mushrooms	onion	zucchini

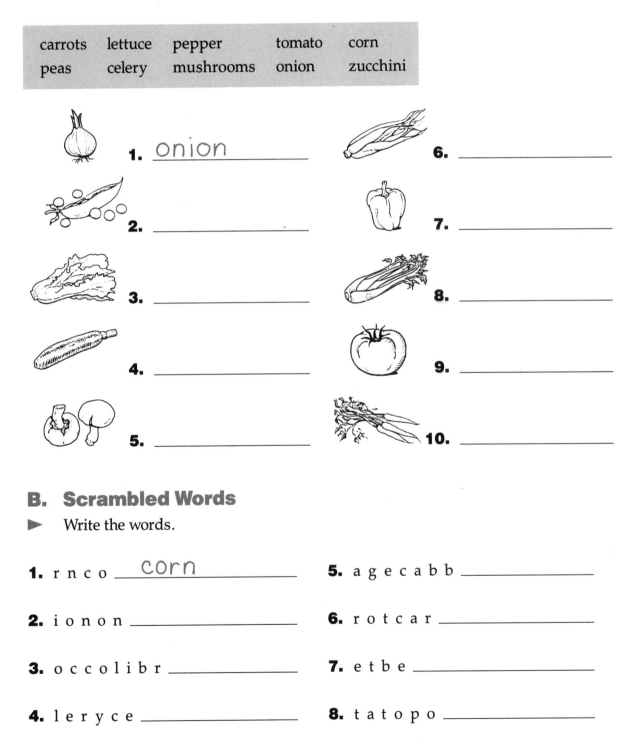

1. onion

2. _____

3. _____

4. _____

5. _____

6. _____

7. _____

8. _____

9. _____

10. _____

B. Scrambled Words

► Write the words.

1. r n c o   corn

2. i o n o n _____

3. o c c o l i b r _____

4. l e r y c e _____

5. a g e c a b b _____

6. r o t c a r _____

7. e t b e _____

8. t a t o p o _____

7

C. Words in Order

▶ Write the words in alphabetical order.

1. spinach   _artichoke_

    artichoke   _spinach_

    yam   _yam_

2. brussels sprouts   _____

    cabbage   _____

    asparagus   _____

3. garlic   _____

    eggplant   _____

    cauliflower   _____

4. turnip   _____

    pumpkin   _____

    radish   _____

A. What Is It?

► Look at the picture.
► Write the word.

orange	lemon	apple	peach
banana	cherries	watermelon	pear

1. watermelon

5. _____

2. _____

6. _____

3. _____

7. _____

4. _____

8. _____

B. Consonants and Vowels

► Circle the words beginning with a vowel.

1. (avocado)   fig   raisin   apricot

2. almonds   pear   plum   date

3. cantaloupe   orange   coconut   hazelnut

C. What's the Word?

▶ Review the words on Dictionary pages 6–7.

▶ Look at the picture.

▶ Fill in the blanks.

▶ Use some of the letters to write the name of another fruit or a vegetable.

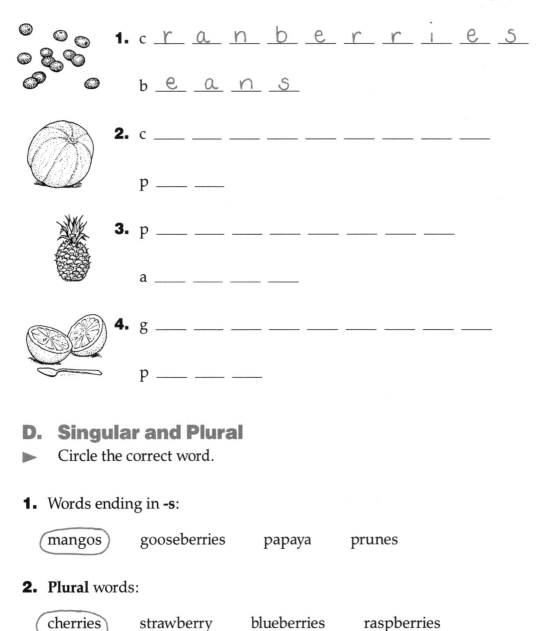

1. c r a n b e r r i e s

   b e a n s

2. c __ __ __ __ __ __ __ __ __

   p __ __

3. p __ __ __ __ __ __ __ __

   a __ __ __ __

4. g __ __ __ __ __ __ __ __ __

   p __ __ __ __

D. Singular and Plural

▶ Circle the correct word.

1. Words ending in **-s**:

(mangos)   gooseberries   papaya   prunes

2. **Plural** words:

(cherries)   strawberry   blueberries   raspberries

3. **Singular** words:

(walnut)   cashews   peanut   almonds

E. What Do You Say?

▶ Choose words to fit in the appropriate categories.

grapes	coconut	fig	plum
grapefruit	lemon	date	pineapple
cherry	strawberry	pear	banana

1. Yellow fruit: _lemon_ _____

_____ _____

_____

2. Sweet yellow fruit: _____ _____

_____

3. Sour yellow fruit: _____ _____

4. Sweet yellow fruit
I like best: _____

A. What Do You See?

► Look at the picture.

► Write the words.

bacon	ham	turkey	ground beef
fish	lobster	lamb chops	chicken legs

1. fish _____

2. _____

3. _____

4. _____

5. _____

6. _____

7. _____

8. _____

B. What's Missing?

► Fill in the blank.

► Write the word.

1. s a ∪ s a g e sausage

2. o __ s t e r _____

3. s t e __ k _____

4. r o __ s t _____

5. b r e __ s t _____

6. t h __ g h _____

12

C. Bingo Bongo

▶ Review the words on Dictionary pages 2–9.

▶ Look for the same words on both the bingo card and the list.

▶ Circle the word on the list.

▶ Cross out the same word on the card.

▶ Cross out five words in a row to win.

Examples of winning cards:

B	I	N	G	O
		●		
		●		
		●		
		●		
		●		

B	I	N	G	O
●				
	●			
		●		
			●	
				●

B	I	N	G	O
				●
			●	
		●		
	●			
●				

B	I	N	G	O
●	●	●	●	●

son	face	broccoli	apple	whole
man	hip	spinach	seed	chicken
woman	chin	lettuce	banana	split
brother	arm	beans	peel	quarter
aunt	leg	tomato	plum	(thigh)
niece	knee	onion	cashew	breast
mother	jaw	garlic	date	roast
father	lip	turnip	blueberries	crab

BINGO CARD				
~~thigh~~	heel	palm	escarole	sister
celery	woman	pod	artichoke	herbs
nephew	baby	seed	parents	elbow
filet	lobster	bacon	onion	yam
corn	avocado	raspberries	chops	hip

6 Containers, Quantities, and Money pages 12–13

A. What Is It?
► Look at the picture.
► Write the word.

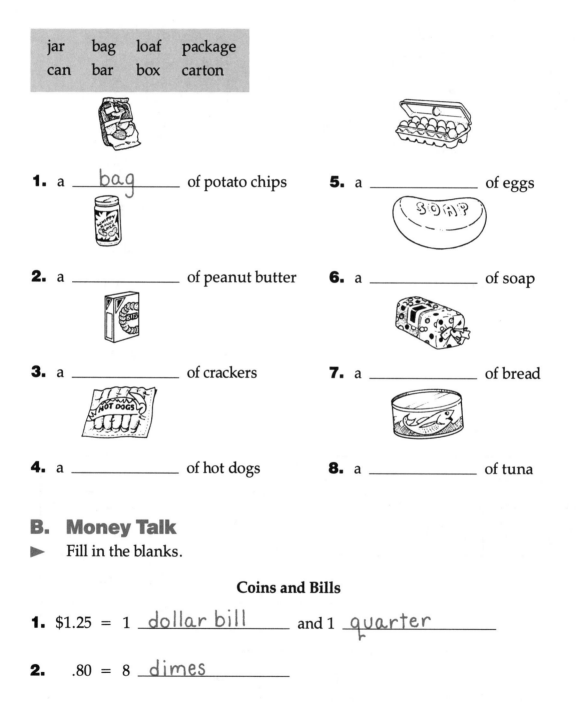

jar	bag	loaf	package
can	bar	box	carton

1. a ___bag___ of potato chips

2. a _____ of peanut butter

3. a _____ of crackers

4. a _____ of hot dogs

5. a _____ of eggs

6. a _____ of soap

7. a _____ of bread

8. a _____ of tuna

B. Money Talk
► Fill in the blanks.

Coins and Bills

1. $1.25 = 1 ___dollar bill___ and 1 ___quarter___

2. .80 = 8 ___dimes___

3. .30 = 6 _____

14

4. .07 = 7 _____

5. .48 = 4 _____, 1 _____,

and 3 _____

6. 3.99 = 3 _____, 3 _____,

2 _____, and 4 _____

7. 10.00 = 10 _____

C. Matching
► Match the **Container** and the **Item**.
► Write a different letter in each blank.

Container	Item
_d_ **1.** a tube	**a.** of coffee
____ **2.** a six-pack	**b.** of pie
____ **3.** a glass	**c.** of soup
____ **4.** a slice	**d.** of toothpaste
____ **5.** a piece	**e.** of pizza
____ **6.** a cup	**f.** of milk
____ **7.** a bowl	**g.** of soda

D. What Goes Together?

► Look at the pictures in the Dictionary.

► Look at the two word lists and decide which foods go with the containers.

► Combine items from each word list to make a shopping list.

container	bar	can	loaf
bottle	roll	tube	box
carton	package	bag	spray can
jar	six-pack	tub	stick

flour	fish	meat	vegetables
toothpaste	coffee	milk	muffins
soda	margarine	eggs	bread
mayonnaise	soap	hot dogs	fruit
soup	peanut butter	aluminum foil	

1 package of hot dogs, 1 six-pack of soda,

_____

_____

_____

_____

_____

7 The Supermarket

A. What's the Answer?

▶ Look at the picture.
▶ Fill in the blanks.
▶ Write the sentence.

| produce | customer | fish | shelf | cash register |

1. I like meat and f __i__ __s__ __h__.

I like meat and fish.

2. The p __ __ __ __ __ __ section

has vegetables and fruit.

3. The cashier is at the c __ __ __

r __ __ __ __ __ __ __ .

4. Canned food is on the s __ __ __ __.

5. The c __ __ __ __ __ __ __

pays with bills and coins.

B. How Many Words?

► Write all the new words you can.
► Check spelling in a larger dictionary.

1. receipt

pit	pet	tip	tree
tire			

2. shopping basket

3. checkout counter

C. Find the Hidden Words

► Find the words.
► Circle each word.
► Write the words.

```
l  q  c  t  m  p  k  i  w  c  k
e  j  u  r  h  o  h  r  h  a  f
t  g  s  g  y  u  i  f  o  s  p
p  d  t  z  s  l  a  x  l  h  x
c  k  o  j  v  t  o  b  b  i  n
i  n  m  i  a  r  p  a  q  e  z
s  h  e  l  f  y  c  d  l  r  u
g  y  r  v  e  h  v  k  s  d  p
```

1. b ___ ___

2. s ___ ___ ___ ___

3. c ___ ___ ___ ___ ___ ___

4. p ___ ___ ___ ___ ___ ___

5. c u s t o m e r

A. What Do You See?

▶ Look at the picture.

▶ Write the words.

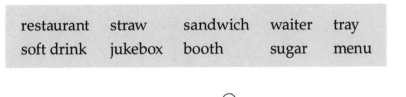

restaurant	straw	sandwich	waiter	tray
soft drink	jukebox	booth	sugar	menu

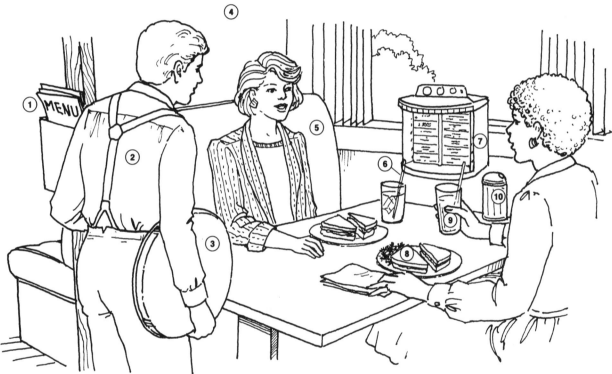

1. ___menu___

2. _____

3. _____

4. _____

5. _____

6. _____

7. _____

8. _____

9. _____

10. _____

B. All the Words

▶ Write the words in alphabetical order.

soft drink	sugar	apron	bar	cork	busboy
ketchup	bar stool	cook	menu	check	sandwich
beer	straw	lighter	tea	pipe	high chair

Words beginning with **b**:

1. _beer_

2. _____

3. _____

4. _____

Words beginning with **c**:

1. _____

2. _____

3. _____

Words beginning with **s**:

1. _____

2. _____

3. _____

4. _____

All the other words:

1. _____

2. _____

3. _____

4. _____

5. _____

6. _____

7. _____

A. What's the Verb?
► Write the verb.

burn   give   pay   cook

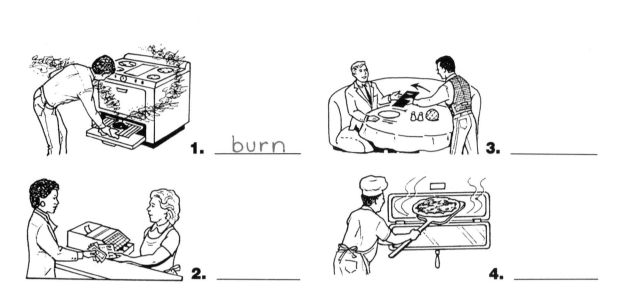

1. <u>burn</u>

3. _____

2. _____

4. _____

B. Scrambled Sentences
► Form a sentence with the words.

1. lunch   waitress   The   is   serving

<u>The waitress is serving lunch.</u>

2. milk   is   drinking   The   baby

_____

3. boy   The   is   eating   sandwich   a

_____

4. is   busboy   the   clearing   The   table

_____

10 Common Prepared Foods page 18

A. What Doesn't Belong?

► Cross out the word that doesn't belong.

Main Course	Other Foods		
fried chicken	mashed potatoes	~~taco~~	biscuit
hamburger	french fries	jelly	bun
eggs	salad dressing	bacon	toast
hot dog	mustard	pickle	egg roll
steak	baked potato	syrup	mixed vegetables

B. Planning Meals

► Plan a sandwich and a drink for lunch.
► Plan the main course for dinner.

	Lunch	Dinner
Monday		
Tuesday		
Wednesday		
Thursday		
Friday		

11 Outdoor Clothes page 19

A. What Is It?

► Look at the picture.

► Write the word.

overcoat	turtleneck sweater	flannel shirt
jacket	V-neck sweater	jeans

1. _flannel shirt_

4. _____

2. _____

5. _____

3. _____

6. _____

B. Matching

► Review the words on Dictionary pages 4-5.

► Match the **Clothes** and the **Part of the Body**.

► Write **a**, **b**, **c**, or **d** in the blanks.

Clothes

Part of the Body

1. _a_ earmuffs

6. ___ boots

a. head

2. ___ tights

7. ___ ski cap

b. hand

3. ___ gloves

8. ___ ice skates

c. leg

4. ___ hat

9. ___ rain boots

d. foot

5. ___ mittens

10. ___ beret

23

12 **Everyday Clothes**   pages 20–21

A. Word Circles

▶ Review the words on Dictionary page **2**.

▶ Circle the words that go with the picture.

1. man (woman) boy girl

hard hat

dress

(suit)

(jacket)

(skirt)

(purse)

tie

(high heels)

2. man woman boy girl

jacket

slacks

briefcase

tie

shirt

sneakers

raincoat

loafers

3. man woman boy girl

pants

sneakers

T-shirt

jacket

blazer

belt

shirt

4. man woman boy girl

dress

cardigan

pants

blouse

skirt

shoes

sneakers

B. What Do You Say?

► Choose words to fit in the appropriate categories.

1. Clothes for men: tie _____   _____

_____   _____   _____

2. Clothes for women: _____   _____

_____   _____   _____

3. My clothes for today: _____   _____

_____   _____   _____

4. Clothes I need to buy: _____   _____

_____   _____   _____

C. True or False

► Look at the picture in the Dictionary.
► Write **True** or **False**.

1. __True__ A runner is wearing a sweatband.

2. _____ A woman is holding a briefcase.

3. _____ A woman with glasses is wearing a uniform.

4. _____ A woman is wearing a hard hat.

5. _____ A man is carrying a lunch box.

6. _____ A boy is wearing a raincoat.

7. _____ A woman is wearing sandals.

13 Underwear and Sleepwear page 22

A. What Do You See?

► Look at the picture.
► Write the words.

boxer shorts	pantyhose	bathrobe	panties	bra
undershirt	nightgown	socks	slip	

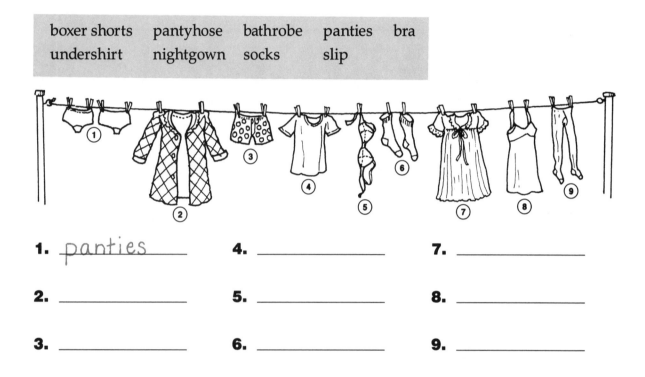

1. panties   **4.** _____   **7.** _____

2. _____   **5.** _____   **8.** _____

3. _____   **6.** _____   **9.** _____

B. Things I Wear

► Write the words from exercise A.

Things I Wear

1. _____

2. _____

3. _____

4. _____

5. _____

Things I Don't Wear

1. _____

2. _____

3. _____

4. _____

5. _____

26

14 Jewelry and Cosmetics page 23

A. What Is It?

► Look at the picture.

► Write the word.

nail clippers	watchband	lipstick	razor	watch
nail polish	necklace	perfume	pin	

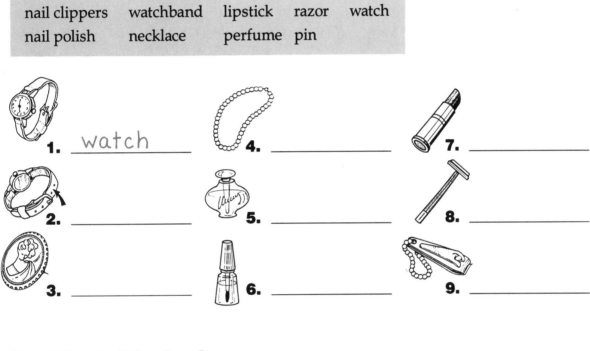

1. watch_____

2. _____

3. _____

4. _____

5. _____

6. _____

7. _____

8. _____

9. _____

B. What's Missing?

► Review the words on Dictionary pages 4–5.

► Fill in the blanks.

► Underline the word for the part of the body.

Cosmetics and Jewelry   **Part of the Body**

1. e _m_ _e_ _r_ _y_ b _o_ _a_ _r_ _d_   head chin fingernail

2. n __ __ __ __ __ __ __   eye neck wrist

3. b __ __ __ __ __ __ __   wrist finger eye

4. m __ __ __ __ __ __   chin head eyelash

5. r __ __ __   finger cheek chin

A. What's the Answer?

▶ Look at the picture.

▶ Write the words.

▶ Write the sentence.

| closed | big | clean | long | small | dirty | short | open |

1. One purse is o ___ ___ ___, and one is

   c ___ ___ ___ ___ ___.

2. One shoe is b ___ ___, and one is

   s ___ ___ ___ ___.

3. One skirt is l ___ ___ ___, and one is

   s ___ ___ ___ ___.

4. One sock is c ___ ___ ___ ___, and one is

   d ___ ___ ___ ___.

B. Going Shopping

▶ Choose which clothes you can buy with each amount.

▶ Describe the clothes with adjectives.

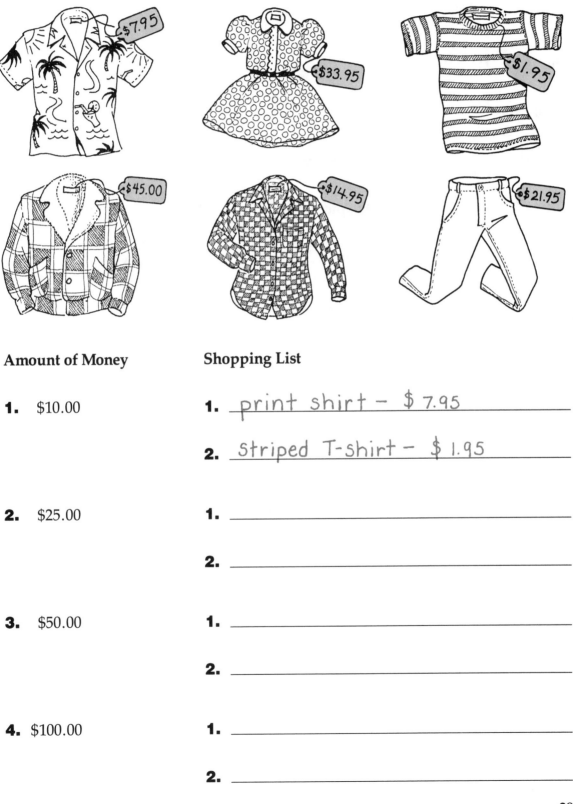

Amount of Money	Shopping List
1. $10.00	**1.** print shirt – $ 7.95
	2. striped T-shirt – $ 1.95
2. $25.00	**1.** _____
	2. _____
3. $50.00	**1.** _____
	2. _____
4. $100.00	**1.** _____
	2. _____

A. What Is the Weather Like Today?

► Fill in the blanks.

This is a t h e r m o m e t e r.

What's the t ___ ___ ___ ___ ___ ___ ___ ___ ___ ___?

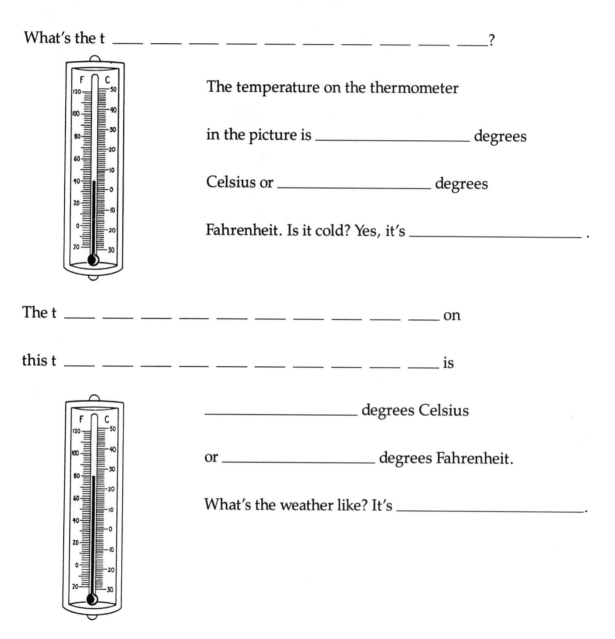

The temperature on the thermometer

in the picture is _____ degrees

Celsius or _____ degrees

Fahrenheit. Is it cold? Yes, it's _____ .

The t ___ ___ ___ ___ ___ ___ ___ ___ ___ ___ on

this t ___ ___ ___ ___ ___ ___ ___ ___ ___ ___ is

_____ degrees Celsius

or _____ degrees Fahrenheit.

What's the weather like? It's _____ .

What's the weather like today? Is it hot, cold, cloudy, rainy, or sunny?

It's _____ .

B. What Should I Wear Today?

▶ Review the words on Dictionary pages **19–22**.

▶ Choose clothes to match the weather.

1. It's hot. _Shorts, sandals_____

2. It's rainy. _____

3. It's snowy. _____

4. It's windy. _____

5. It's sunny. _____

6. It's cool. _____

C. Matching

▶ Match the **Adjective** and its **Opposite**.

▶ Write a different letter in each blank.

	Adjective		**Opposite**
1.	____ wet	**a.**	hot
2.	____ cold	**b.**	dry
3.	____ warm	**c.**	sunny
4.	____ cloudy	**d.**	cool

17 Seasonal Verbs page 26

A. What's the Verb?

▶ Write the verb.

clean	mow	push	carry	pick	dig

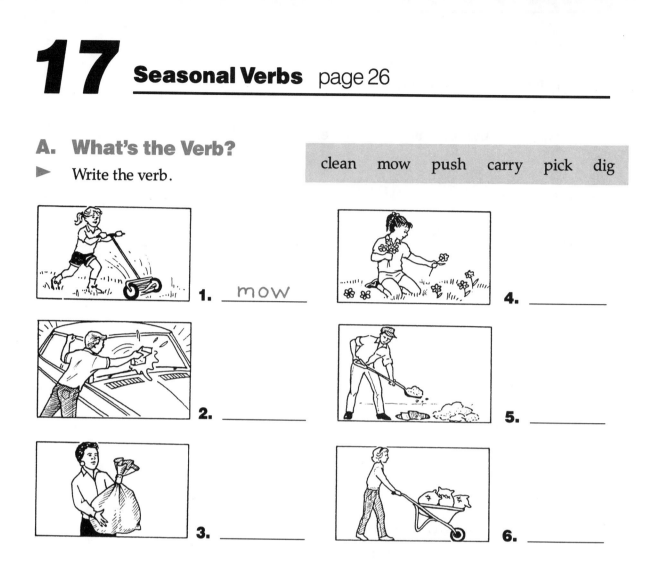

1. <u>mow</u>

2. _____

3. _____

4. _____

5. _____

6. _____

B. What's Happening?

▶ Look at the pictures in the Dictionary.

▶ Answer the questions.

1. What is the woman doing with the trowel?

   She <u>is digging a hole with the trowel.</u>

2. What is the man on the ladder doing with the paintbrush?

   He _____

3. What is the girl doing with the rake?

   She _____

4. What is the boy doing with the shovel?

He _____

5. What is the man doing with the garden hose?

He _____

C. Matching
▶ Review the words on Dictionary pages 19–21.
▶ Match **Clothes** and **Seasons**.
▶ Write **a**, **b**, or **c** in the blanks.

Clothes	**Seasons**
1. ____ raincoat	**a.** spring, summer
2. ____ ski cap	**b.** fall, winter
3. ____ sweatshirt	**c.** spring, summer, fall, and winter
4. ____ shorts	
5. ____ mittens	
6. ____ short-sleeved dress	

A. What Is It?

► Look at the picture.

► Write the word.

shovel	lawn mower	rake	watering can
window	wheelbarrow	grill	garden hose

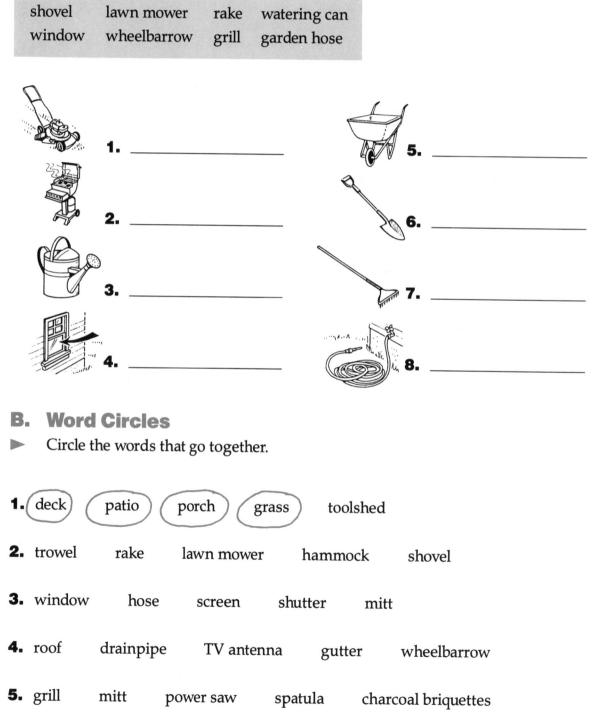

1. _____

2. _____

3. _____

4. _____

5. _____

6. _____

7. _____

8. _____

B. Word Circles

► Circle the words that go together.

1. (deck) (patio) (porch) (grass) toolshed

2. trowel rake lawn mower hammock shovel

3. window hose screen shutter mitt

4. roof drainpipe TV antenna gutter wheelbarrow

5. grill mitt power saw spatula charcoal briquettes

19 Prepositions of Description page 102*

A. Where Are the Tools?

► Look at the picture of the backyard on Dictionary page 27.

► Underline the correct preposition and write the sentence.

1. There are tools (in, on) the toolshed.

There are tools in the toolshed.

2. There is meat cooking (on, in) the grill.

_____

3. There is a lawn mower (above, next to) the house.

_____

4. There is a hammock (on top of, between) the trees.

_____

5. The watering can is (next to, between) the charcoal.

_____

B. True or False

► Look at the pictures of houses on Dictionary page 27.

► Write **True** or **False**.

1. __True_____ The antenna is above the house.

2. _____ The garage is under the driveway.

3. _____ The deck is next to the house.

4. _____ The driveway is behind the house.

5. _____ The porch is in front of the house.

*See also Lesson 75.

35

20 The Living Room page 28

A. What Is It?

► Look at the picture.
► Write the word.

| bookcase | ceiling fan | fireplace | desk | sofa | lamp |

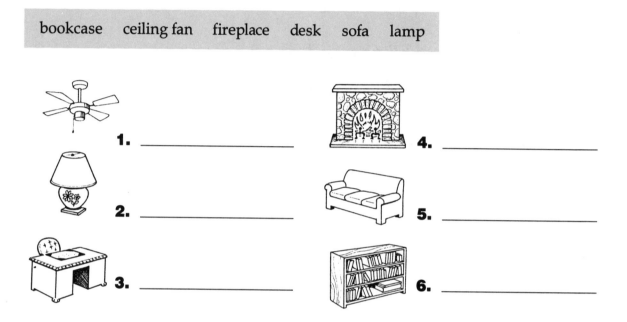

1. _____

2. _____

3. _____

4. _____

5. _____

6. _____

B. All the Words

► Write the words in alphabetical order.

| step | speaker | ceiling | cushion | coffee table |
| sofa | television | carpeting | fireplace | staircase |

Words beginning with **c**:

1. _____

2. _____

3. _____

4. _____

Words beginning with **s**:

1. _____

2. _____

3. _____

4. _____

36

21 The Dining Room page 29

A. What Do You See?

► Look at the picture.
► Write the words.

salt shaker	napkin	glass	knife	cup
saucer	plate	spoon	fork	

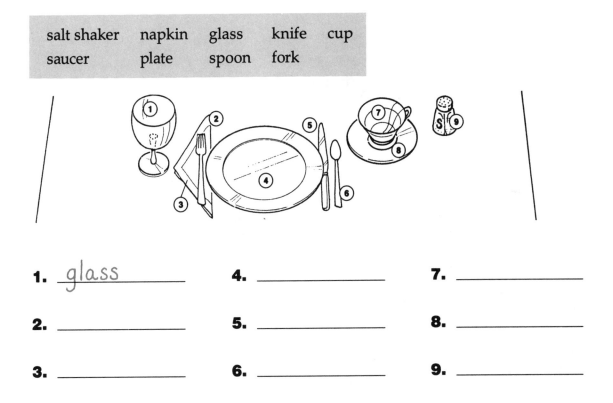

1. _glass_

2. _____

3. _____

4. _____

5. _____

6. _____

7. _____

8. _____

9. _____

B. True or False

► Look at the picture in the Dictionary.
► Write **True** or **False**.

1. _True_ There is china in the china closet.

2. _____ The man is filling water glasses from a teapot.

3. _____ There is a vase with flowers on the chandelier.

4. _____ The silverware is in the buffet.

5. _____ There are no candles in the candlesticks.

A. What Do You See?

► Look at the picture.
► Write the word.

mixing bowl	lid	canister
rolling pin	pot holder	can opener
cutting board	casserole dish	frying pan

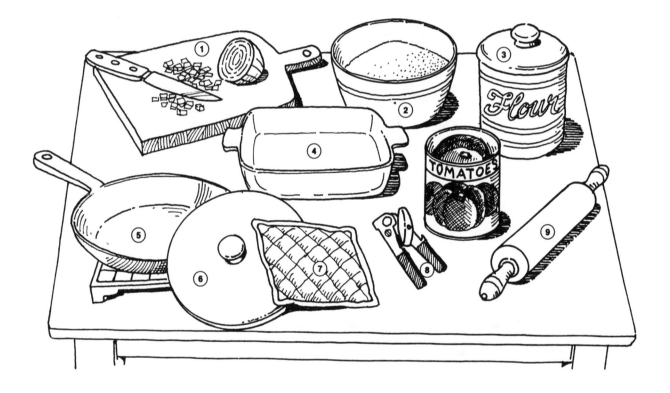

1. cutting board   **4.** _____   **7.** _____

2. _____   **5.** _____   **8.** _____

3. _____   **6.** _____   **9.** _____

B. Where's the Coffee Maker?

▶ Look at the picture in the Dictionary.

▶ Underline the correct answer.

▶ Write the sentence.

1. The coffee maker is on the (ceiling, counter, <u>stove</u>).

The coffee maker is on the stove.

2. The rolling pin is on the (shelf, counter, stove).

_____

3. The pots and pans are on the (shelf, counter, wall).

_____

4. The dish towel is on the (shelf, refrigerator, wall).

_____

5. The casserole dish is in the (stove, cabinet, refrigerator).

_____

6. The blender is on the (counter, shelf, stove).

_____

7. The dishes are in the (freezer, stove, dishwasher).

_____

8. The ice tray is in the (freezer, cabinet, dishwasher).

_____

23 Kitchen Verbs page 31

A. What's the Verb?

► Write the verb.

| break   peel   cut   boil   open   pour |

 1. <u>boil</u>

2. _____

3. _____

4. _____

5. _____

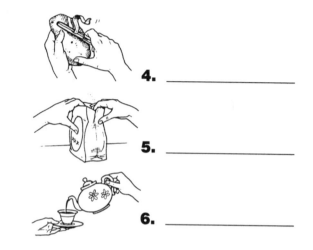 6. _____

B. A Recipe

► Circle the verbs.

```
                         Apple Crisp


Turn oven to 350 degrees.


Spread 1 teaspoon margarine in a small baking pan.
Peel 5 cooking apples, cut into quarters, and slice
   into pan.
Mix 1/3 cup each flour and sugar in a small bowl
   with 1 1/2 cups granola and 1 teaspoon cinnamon.
Pour 1/4 cup melted butter into the flour mixture,
   stir, and spread over apples.


Bake about 25 minutes                    Serves 16.
```

40

C. How Can You Open a Can?

► Review the words on Dictionary pages 29–30.

► Look at the pictures in the Dictionary.

► Fill in the blanks.

► Write the sentence.

1. She ___stirs___ the coffee with a ___spoon___ .

___She stirs the coffee with a spoon.___

2. She _____ the carrots with a vegetable peeler.

_____

3. He _____ the turkey with a _____ .

_____

4. He _____ the can with a _____ .

_____

5. She _____ the eggs with an egg beater.

_____

6. She _____ the onions with a _____ .

_____

41

24 The Bedroom page 32

A. What Do You See?
▶ Look at the picture.
▶ Write the words.

pillow	sheet	bed	comforter	headboard
blanket	floor	rug	mattress	

1. <u>headboard</u>   4. _____   7. _____

2. _____   5. _____   8. _____

3. _____   6. _____   9. _____

B. Word Circles
▶ Circle the words that go together.

1. (chest of drawers)   (mirror)   blinds   (bureau)   (night table)

2. bed   headboard   rug   mattress   box spring

3. closet   comb   hanger   hook   clothes

4. pillow   pillowcase   sheet   blanket   alarm clock

5. jack   cord   phone   light switch

42

A. What Goes In the Toy Chest?

▶ Choose words to fit in the appropriate categories.

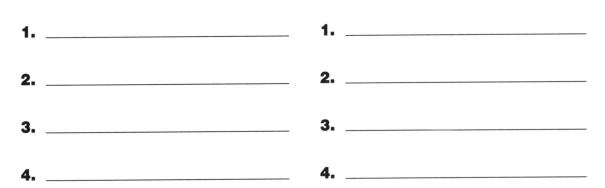

| baby lotion | baby wipes | block | disposable diaper |
| baby powder | teddy bear | doll | rattle |

Toys

1. _____

2. _____

3. _____

4. _____

Things You Use to Change a Baby

1. _____

2. _____

3. _____

4. _____

B. A Crossword Puzzle

▶ Look at the pictures.

▶ Complete the words.

Across:

Down:

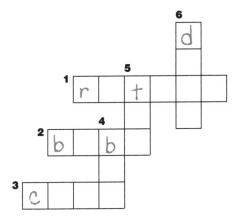

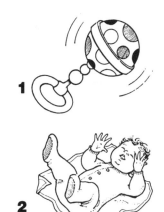

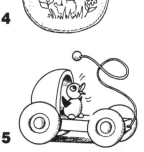

26 The Bathroom page 34

A. What Is It?

► Look at the picture.

► Write the word.

medicine chest	bathtub	shower head
wastepaper basket	sink	scale

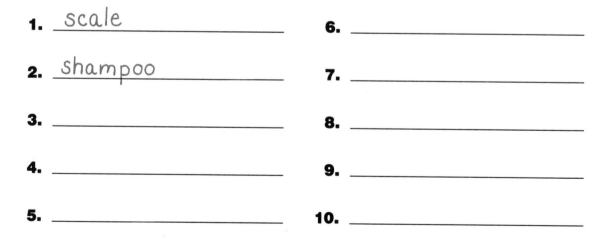

1. _sink_

2. _____

3. _____

4. _____

5. _____

6. _____

B. Words in Order

► Look at the words in the Dictionary.

► Write in alphabetical order the words beginning with **s**.

1. _scale_

2. _shampoo_

3. _____

4. _____

5. _____

6. _____

7. _____

8. _____

9. _____

10. _____

C. What's Different?

► Fill in the blanks.

► Circle the word ending in different letters.

1. f a u c ___ ___   t o w ___ ___   t o i l ___ ___

2. soap   d i ___ ___   w a s h c l o ___ ___   t o o t h b r u ___ ___

3. hair   d r y ___ ___   h a m p ___ ___   b a t h t ___ ___

A. What Is It?

► Look at the picture.

► Write the word.

ironing board	broom	mop	clothespins	vacuum cleaner
bucket	washing machine	dryer	flashlight	lightbulb

1. _dryer_

2. _____

3. _____

4. _____

5. _____

6. _____

7. _____

8. _____

9. _____

10. _____

B. What's Missing?

► Fill in the blanks.

► Write the word.

1. l a _u_ n d r y b a s _k_ e t   _laundry basket_

2. f e ___ t h e r d u s ___ e r   _____

3. g a r b a ___ e c ___ n   _____

4. v a c u ___ m   c l e ___ n e r   _____

5. p ___ p e r   t o w ___ l s   _____

6. l a ___ n d r y   d e t e r ___ e n t _____

7. c i r c u ___ t   b r e ___ k e r   _____

8. f a b ___ i c   s o f ___ e n e r   _____

C. You're the Artist

▶ Draw a floor plan of a house.

▶ Write the names of the rooms on the plan.

▶ Include a utility room.

A. What Is It?

► Look at the picture.
► Write the word.

hatchet	wood plane	pliers	electric drill	plug
wrench	hammer	vise	mallet	

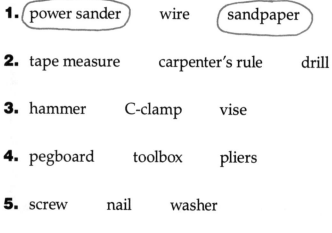

1. vise

4. _____

7. _____

2. _____

5. _____

8. _____

3. _____

6. _____

9. _____

B. Word Circles

► Circle the words that go together.

1. (power sander)   wire   (sandpaper)

2. tape measure   carpenter's rule   drill

3. hammer   C-clamp   vise

4. pegboard   toolbox   pliers

5. screw   nail   washer

C. What's the Answer?

► Look at the picture.
► Fill in the blanks.
► Write the sentence.

1. You can paint wood with a

p __ __ __ __ __ __ __ __ .

_____

2. You can cut wood with a s __ __ .

_____

3. You can hold wood together with g __ __ __ .

_____

4. You can measure wood with a t __ __ __

m __ __ __ __ __ __ .

_____

_____

A. Matching

► Match **Activity** and **Object**.

► Write a different letter in each blank.

Activity

1. _C_ change
2. _e_ dry
3. ___ scrub
4. ___ oil
5. ___ repair
6. ___ wash
7. ___ dust

Object

a. the car
b. the toaster
c. the sheets
d. the furniture
e. the clothes
f. the floor
g. the lawn mower

B. What Do You Do on Saturdays?

► Choose a verb for each time of day.

► Try to use verbs from page 38.

1. 6:00 a.m. _I sleep._
2. 7:00 _____
3. 8:00 _____
4. 9:00 _I make the bed._
5. 10:00 _____
6. 11:00 _____
7. 12:00 _____

8. 1:00 p.m. _____
9. 2:00 _____
10. 3:00 _____
11. 5:00 _____
12. 6:00 _____
13. 7:00 _____
14. 8:00 _____

30 **Medical and Dental Care** page 39

A. **What's the Answer?**

► Look at the pictures in the Dictionary.

► Fill in the blanks.

► Write the sentence.

doctor	cast	sling	examining table
nurse	stitches	patient	

1. The p __a__ __t__ __i__ __e__ __n__ __t__ is in the hospital.

The patient is in the hospital.

2. The d ___ ___ ___ ___ ___ examines the patient.

_____

3. The patient is on the e ___ ___ ___ ___ ___ ___ ___ ___

t ___ ___ ___ ___.

_____

_____

4. The n ___ ___ ___ ___ helps the patient.

_____

5. Her arm is in a s ___ ___ ___ ___.

_____

51

6. Her leg is in a c ____ ____ ____ .

_____

7. The little boy has s ____ ____ ____ ____ ____ ____ ____ in his head.

_____

B. Matching

► Match the **Person** with the **Instrument**.

► Write a different letter in each blank.

Person	Instrument
1. ____ doctor	**a.** stretcher
2. ____ dentist	**b.** stethoscope
3. ____ nurse	**c.** needle
4. ____ attendant	**d.** drill

C. Word Circles

► Circle the words that go together.

1. patient   attendant   oral hygienist   nurse

2. cast   stethoscope   crutch   sling

3. stretcher   wheelchair   examining table   pedal

4. bandage   syringe   Band-Aid   gauze pads

A. Words in Order

▶ Write the words in alphabetical order.

rash	infection	fever	chills
cold	cut	burn	bruise

1. <u>bruise</u>

2. _____

3. _____

4. _____

5. _____

6. _____

7. _____

8. _____

B. Where Does It Hurt?

▶ Fill in the blanks.

backache	sore throat	headache	toothache

1. My head hurts. I have a h <u>e</u> <u>a</u> <u>d</u> <u>a</u> <u>c</u> <u>h</u> <u>e</u> .

2. My tooth hurts. I have a t ___ ___ ___ ___ ___ ___ ___ ___ .

3. My throat hurts. I have a s ___ ___ ___ t ___ ___ ___ ___ ___ .

4. My back hurts. I have a b ___ ___ ___ ___ ___ ___ ___ .

C. What Do You Need?

► Underline the correct treatment or remedy.

1. I need   (<u>an ice pack</u>, ointment)   for a sprain.

2. I need   (eye drops, a stretch bandage)   for an eye infection.

3. I need   (eye drops, ointment)   for a rash.

4. I need   (an ice pack, pills)   for a sore throat.

5. I need   (a stretch bandage, pills)   for a headache.

6. I need   (bed rest, surgery)   for a cold.

D. How Many Words?

► Write all the new words you can.
► Check spelling in a larger dictionary.

1. high blood pressure

sure	dog	good	press
hide	rode		

2. tongue depressor

3. stretch bandage

54

A. What Do You See?

► Look at the picture.

► Write the words.

hose	fire engine	water	fire fighter	ambulance
fire	fire hydrant	fire escape	fire extinguisher	smoke

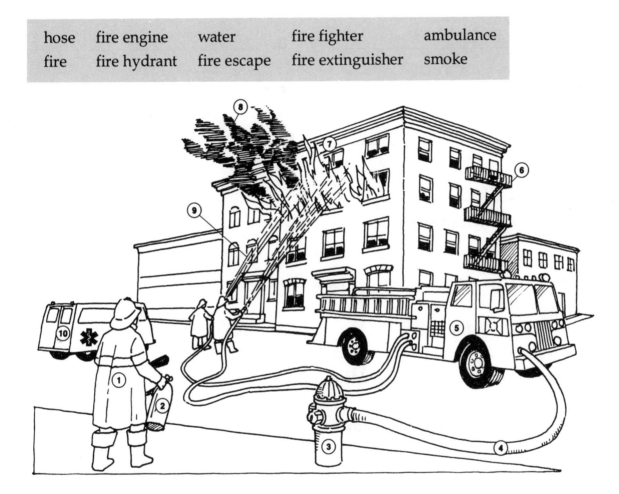

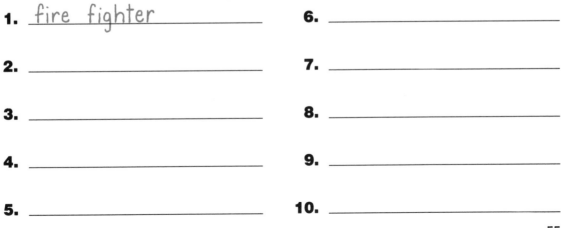

1. <u>fire fighter</u>

2. _____

3. _____

4. _____

5. _____

6. _____

7. _____

8. _____

9. _____

10. _____

B. Words in Order

▶ Write the words from exercise A in alphabetical order.

1. _ambulance_   6. _____

2. _____   7. _____

3. _____   8. _____

4. _____   9. _____

5. _____   10. _____

C. Word Circles

▶ Circle the words that go together.

1. hose   nozzle   water   ladder

2. fire truck   fire engine   ax   ambulance

3. fire   ax   hose   ladder

4. fire   coat   water   smoke

A. What Is It?

► Look at the picture.
► Write the words.

fingerprints	police officer	judge
holster	gun	handcuffs

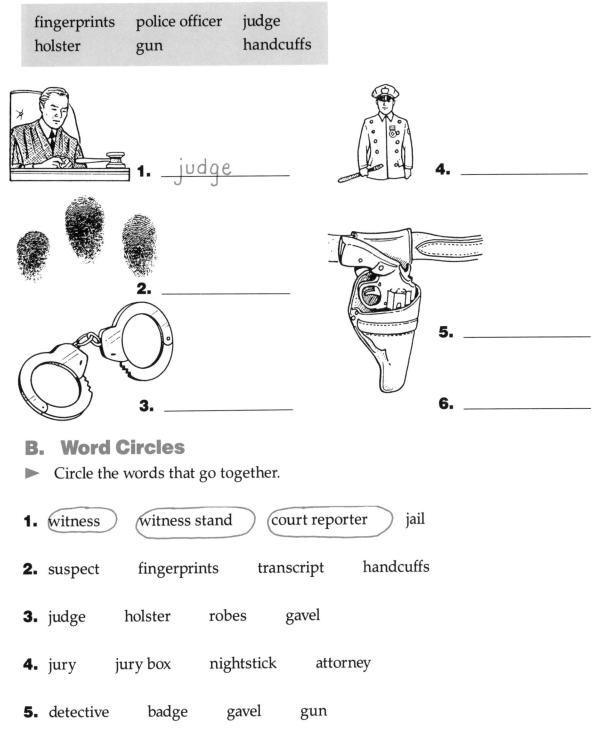

1. _judge_

2. _____

3. _____

4. _____

5. _____

6. _____

B. Word Circles

► Circle the words that go together.

1. (witness) (witness stand) (court reporter) jail

2. suspect   fingerprints   transcript   handcuffs

3. judge   holster   robes   gavel

4. jury   jury box   nightstick   attorney

5. detective   badge   gavel   gun

C. Where Did It Happen, Officer?

► Review the words on Dictionary pages 26–30.

► Underline the place.

1. The suspect took a garden hose, a lawn mower, and a rake.

    a. The backyard

    b. The kitchen

    c. The bathroom

2. The suspect took a pearl necklace, earrings, and a watch.

    a. The kitchen

    b. The bedroom

    c. The living room

3. The suspect took a television and a stereo.

    a. The dining room

    b. The living room

    c. The bedroom

4. The suspect took spoons, forks, knives, and a teapot.

    a. The dining room

    b. The living room

    c. The bedroom

A. What's the Answer?

▶ Look at the picture in the Dictionary.
▶ Fill in the blanks.
▶ Write the sentence.

| traffic light | intersection | pedestrians | elevator |
| corner | street sign | sidewalk | |

1. The traffic cop stands in the

i n t e r s e c t i o n.

The traffic cop stands in the intersection.

2. The t _ _ _ _ _ _ l _ _ _ _ is on the

c _ _ _ _ _ .

_____

3. The s _ _ _ _ _ s _ _ _ is near the post office.

_____

4. The parking garage has an e _ _ _ _ _ _ _ .

_____

5. Many p _ _ _ _ _ _ _ _ _ _ are walking

on the street.

_____

6. People walk on the s _ _ _ _ _ _ _ .

B. Relationships

► Fill in the blanks.

1. apartment house: apartment — office building: ___office___

___Apartment house___ is to ___apartment___ as

___office building___ is to ___office___ .

2. subway station: subway — bus stop: _____

_____ is to _____ as

_____ is to _____ .

3. bookstore: books — newsstand: _____

_____ is to _____ as

_____ is to _____ .

C. What Can You Buy at a Bookstore?

► Answer with one or two words.

1. What can you buy at a bookstore? _____

2. At a fruit and vegetable market? _____

3. At a bakery? _____

4. At a drugstore? _____

5. At a newsstand? _____

35 Prepositions of Motion   page 103*

A. What's Missing?

► Fill in the blank.
► Write the word.

1. o __v__ e r   _over_

2. f r ___ m   _____

3. a r o ___ n d   _____

4. t o ___ a r d   _____

5. t h r o u g ___   _____

6. a w a ___ f r o m   _____

B. Where Are They Going?

► Look at the picture on Dictionary pages **44–45**.
► Fill in the blanks.

| out of | up | into | across | down |

1. The woman is going _____ the subway stairs.

2. The man is going _____ the subway stairs.

3. The man is going _____ the drugstore.

4. The man in the wheelchair is going _____ the street.

5. A man is going _____ the post office.

A. What Do You See?

► Look at the pictures.

► Write the words.

zip code	postmark	package	money order	stamp
address	envelope	return address	mailbox	label

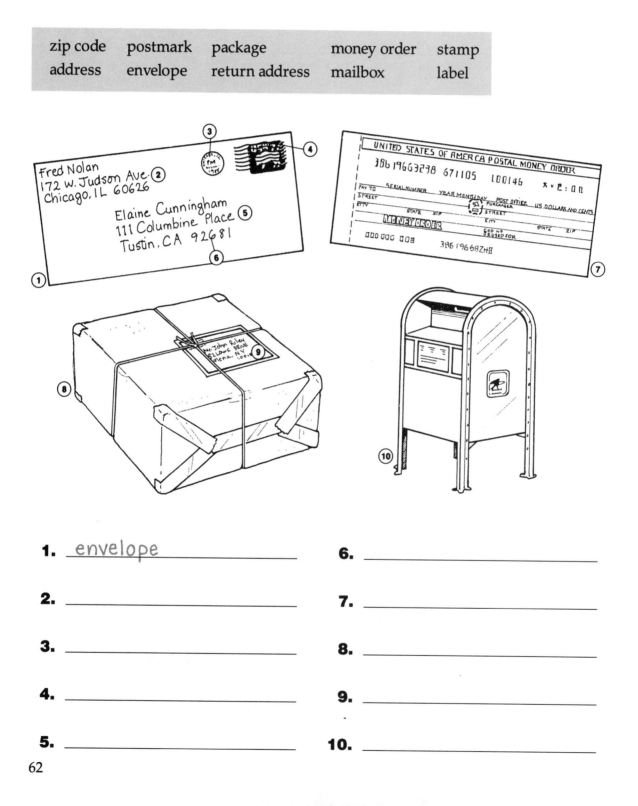

1. _envelope_

2. _____

3. _____

4. _____

5. _____

6. _____

7. _____

8. _____

9. _____

10. _____

B. Word Circles

► Circle the words that go together.

1. airmail   Express Mail   mailbag

2. mail truck   mailbox   stamp

3. window   postcard   letter

4. postal worker   letter   letter carrier

5. zip code   string   tape

C. What Do You Need?

► Complete the sentence.

What do you need to mail a package? List the items.

I need _____

_____

D. Address an Envelope

► Address an envelope to a friend.
► Label all the parts.

A. What's the Answer?

▶ Look at the picture in the Dictionary.

▶ Fill in the blanks.

▶ Write the sentence.

periodicals section	information desk	card catalog	magazines
photocopy machine	library card	library	globe

1. Many people go to the l ___ ___ ___ ___ ___ ___ every day.

_____

2. You ask for help at the i ___ ___ ___ ___ ___ ___ ___ ___ ___

d ___ ___ ___ .

_____

_____

3. You can make a copy on the p ___ ___ ___ ___ ___ ___ ___ ___

m ___ ___ ___ ___ ___ ___ .

_____

_____

4. There is a g ___ ___ ___ ___ on the table near the bookshelves.

_____

5. People read m __ __ __ __ __ __ __ __ in the

 p __ __ __ __ __ __ __ __ __ __

 s __ __ __ __ __ __ .

_____

_____

6. You look for a book title in the c __ __ __

 c __ __ __ __ __ __ .

_____

_____

7. You show your l __ __ __ __ __ __   c __ __ __

 to take a book home.

_____

_____

B. Who's the Author?
► Look at one of your books.
► Answer the questions.

1. What's the title? _____

2. Who's the author? _____

C. Where Can I Find It?

► Match **Item** and **Place in the Library**.

► Write a different letter in each blank.

Item	**Place in the Library**
1. ____ the call number of a book	**a.** information desk
2. ____ a magazine	**b.** dictionary
3. ____ how to spell a word	**c.** card catalog
4. ____ a map of the United States	**d.** atlas
5. ____ information	**e.** periodicals section

D. Index

► Look in the index of the Dictionary.

► On what page(s) do you find these words?

atlas _____   globe _____   dictionary _____

gutter _____   sprinkler _____   shovel _____

log _____   vase _____   painting _____

fork _____   salt shaker _____ pitcher _____

canister _____   steamer _____   broiler _____

A. Doubles

▶ Write all the words with double letters.

periscope	ammunition	cannon	bullet
trigger	battleship	shell	parachute
bomb	personnel	rifle	jeep

	Word	Double Letter		Word	Double Letter
1.	ammunition	mm	5.		
2.			6.		
3.			7.		
4.			8.		

B. What Doesn't Belong?

▶ Cross out the word that doesn't belong.

Vehicles	jeep	~~rifle~~	bomber	submarine
Weapons	bullet	sailor	shell	mortar
Personnel	battleship	airman	soldier	marine
Armed Forces	Air Force	Army	tank	Navy

A. **What Do You See?**

► Look at the picture.

► Write the words.

tractor trailer	pickup truck	panel truck
tow truck	flatbed	dump truck

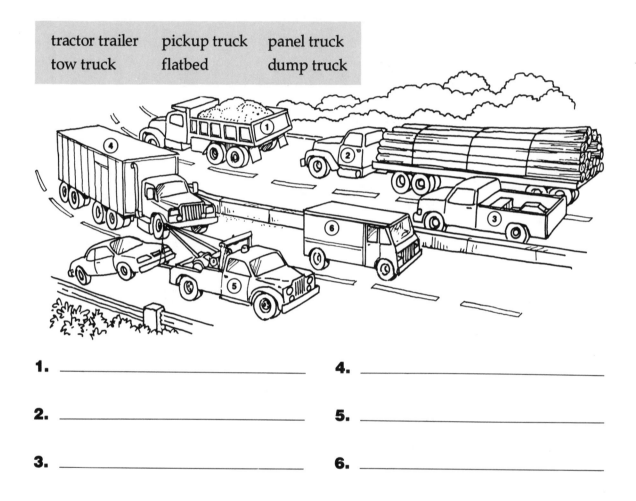

1. _____

2. _____

3. _____

4. _____

5. _____

6. _____

B. **What Do You Think?**

► Look at the picture in the Dictionary.

► Say which truck carries each item. There may be more than one correct answer.

1. garbage _____

2. cement _____

3. food _____

4. sand _____

5. furniture _____

6. cars _____

40 Cars pages 50–51

A. What Is It?
▶ Look at the picture.
▶ Write the word.

| station wagon | gas gauge | sedan |
| steering wheel | speedometer | hatchback |

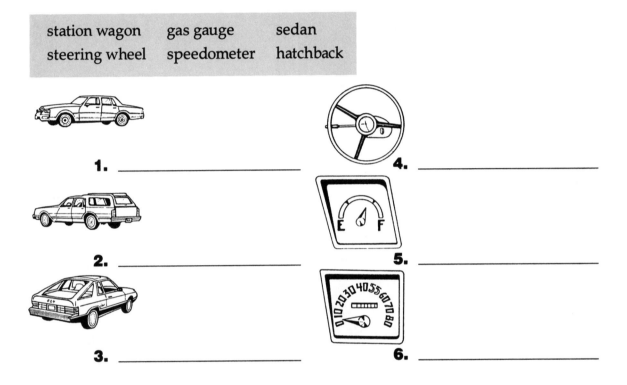

1. _____

2. _____

3. _____

4. _____

5. _____

6. _____

B. What's Missing?
▶ Fill in the blank.
▶ Write the word.

1. i g n i ___ i o n   _____

2. a c ___ e l e r a t o r   _____

3. b a t t ___ r y   _____

4. e n g i n ___   _____

5. c l u ___ c h   _____

C. You're the Artist

► Draw and label all the parts.
► Write the words on the picture.

1. hood
2. trunk
3. tire
4. bumper
5. antenna

6. windshield wiper
7. windshield
8. headlight
9. rear light
10. headrest

D. Find the Hidden Words

► Find the words.
► Circle each word.
► Write the words.

```
w  i  n  d  s  h  i  e  l  d  b  e
t  l  h  n  d  e  b  g  w  u  s  b
i  p  k  v  r  a  d  i  a  t  o  r
r  s  r  u  o  d  p  t  l  g  n  a
e  x  w  q  c  l  s  w  a  c  f  k
h  x  b  r  l  i  s  w  p  w  m  e
r  x  j  k  t  g  m  s  m  r  l  t
u  z  g  i  k  h  o  o  d  a  i  f
x  b  d  w  y  t  m  u  v  e  j  s
```

1. h ___ ___ ___

2. t ___ ___ ___

3. b ___ ___ ___ ___

4. r ___ ___ ___ ___ ___ ___ ___

5. h ___ ___ ___ ___ ___ ___ ___

6. w ___ ___ ___ ___ ___ ___ ___ ___ ___

41 Bikes page 52

A. What Do You See?

► Look at the picture.
► Write the words.

handlebars	reflector	fender	pedal	seat
hand brake	bicycle	wheel	chain	pump

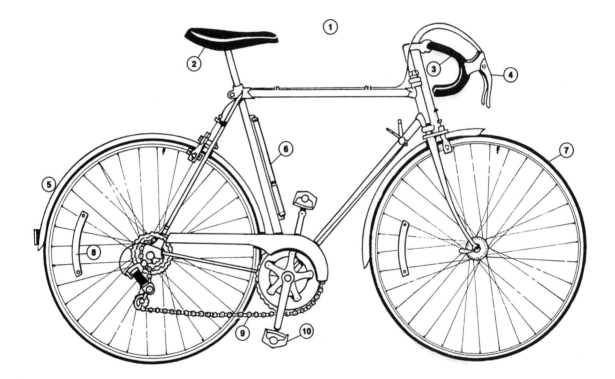

1. _____
2. _____
3. _____
4. _____
5. _____

6. _____
7. _____
8. _____
9. _____
10. _____

B. Types of Bikes

▶ Choose words to fit in the appropriate categories.

Bikes for Children

1. _____

2. _____

3. _____

Bikes for Adults

1. _____

2. _____

3. _____

Bikes With Motors

1. _____

2. _____

3. _____

Bikes for the Highway

1. _____

2. _____

3. _____

C. On the Safe Side

▶ List items for safety.

1. _____

2. _____

3. _____

4. _____

5. _____

6. _____

7. _____

8. _____

A. What Do You See?

► Look at the picture.

► Write the words.

trailer	interstate highway	right lane	left lane	van
gas pump	overpass	motorcycle	sports car	service area

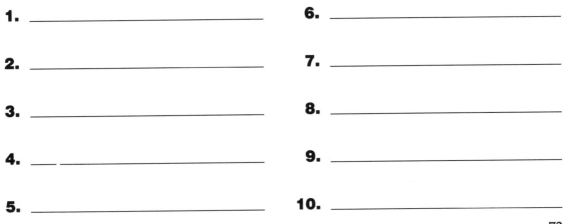

1. _____

2. _____

3. _____

4. _____

5. _____

6. _____

7. _____

8. _____

9. _____

10. _____

B. Words in Order

▶ Write the words in alphabetical order.

shoulder	exit ramp	tollbooth	attendant
hitchhiker	passenger car	camper	road sign

1. _____   5. _____

2. _____   6. _____

3. _____   7. _____

4. _____   8. _____

C. What's the Answer?

▶ Look at the picture in the Dictionary.

▶ Fill in the blanks.

▶ Write the sentence.

1. The car entered the s ___ ___ ___ ___ ___ ___ a ___ ___ ___ .

_____

2. The driver asked the a ___ ___ ___ ___ ___ ___ ___ ___

to fill up the gas tank.

_____

_____

3. The attendant went to the g ___ ___ p ___ ___ ___ .

_____

74

A. What's the Answer?

▶ Look at the picture.

▶ Fill in the blanks.

▶ Write the sentence.

passenger	bus driver	commuter train
cable car	subway platform	

1. The b ___ ___   d ___ ___ ___ ___ ___ is

giving the rider a transfer.

_____

2. The rider is waiting on the s ___ ___ ___ ___ ___

p ___ ___ ___ ___ ___ ___ ___ .

_____

3. The c ___ ___ ___ ___ ___ ___ ___

t ___ ___ ___ ___ is in the station.

_____

4. The p __ __ __ __ __ __ __ __

is giving the cab driver a tip.

5. I would like to ride on a c __ __ __ __

c __ __ .

B. True or False

▶ Look at the pictures in the Dictionary.

▶ Write **True** or **False**.

1. _____ The rider is putting his fare in the fare box.

2. _____ The subway rider is hanging on to the turnstile.

3. _____ The commuter train is waiting on the track.

4. _____ The passenger is getting into the taxicab.

5. _____ The horse-drawn carriage has an engine.

C. What Do You Say?

▶ Review the words on Dictionary page **103**.

▶ Choose the public transportation for each trip.

1. Across the city: _____

2. To another city: _____

76

A. What Is It?

► Look at the picture.

► Write the word.

| pilot | suitcase | ticket |
| flight attendant | porter | boarding pass |

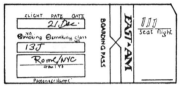

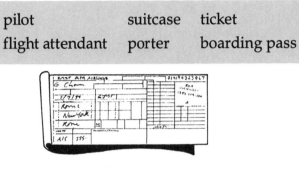

1. _____

4. _____

2. _____

5. _____

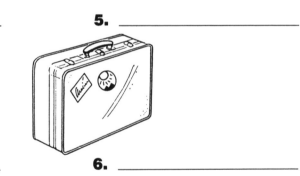

3. _____

6. _____

B. What Doesn't Belong?

► Cross out the word that doesn't belong.

Person	traveler	metal detector	flight engineer	copilot
Place	cabin	aisle	cockpit	dolly
Object	tray table	security guard	x-ray screener	instruments

A. What Is It?

► Look at the picture.
► Write the word.

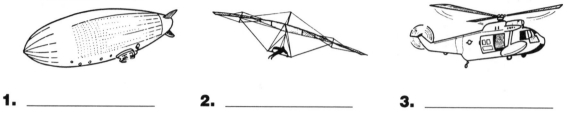

1. _____   **2.** _____   **3.** _____

B. You're the Artist

► Draw and label parts of a jet plane.
► Write the words on the picture.

1. wing

2. jet engine

3. fuselage

4. landing gear

5. tail

6. nose

C. Word Circles

► Circle the words that go together.

1. jet engine   fuselage   runway   wing

2. control tower   tail   terminal building   hangar

3. blimp   propeller plane   glider   nose

78

A. **What Do You See?**

► Look at the picture.
► Write the words.

smokestack	cargo	hold	bow
anchor	deck	line	

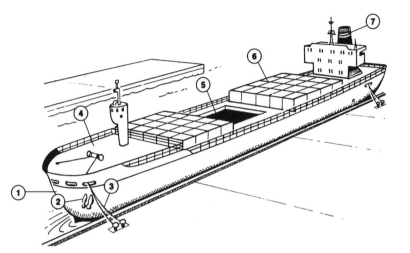

1. _____   5. _____

2. _____   6. _____

3. _____   7. _____

4. _____

B. **How Many Words?**

► Write all the new words you can.
► Check spelling in a larger dictionary.

1. lighthouse _____ _____ _____ _____

_____ _____ _____ _____

2. fisherman _____ _____ _____ _____

_____ _____ _____ _____

47 **Pleasure Boating** page 59

A. What Is It?

► Look at the picture.

► Write the word.

| sailboat | motorboat | canoe | dinghy | kayak | rowboat |

1. _____

2. _____

3. _____

4. _____

5. _____

6. _____

B. What Do You Say?

► Look at the pictures on Dictionary pages **58–59**.

► Choose boats to match each description.

1. Fast boat: _____

2. Slow boat: _____

3. Big boat: _____

4. Small boat: _____

5. Narrow boat: _____

48 Plants and Trees pages 60–61

A. What Is It?

► Look at the picture.

► Write the word.

rose	daffodil	violet	poinsettia	tulip
daisy	buttercup	mum	sunflower	

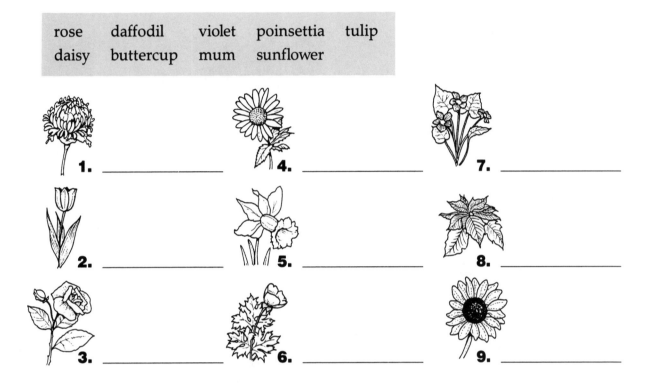

1. _____
4. _____
7. _____

2. _____
5. _____
8. _____

3. _____
6. _____
9. _____

B. Word Circles

► Circle the words that go together.

1. poison sumac   cone   poison ivy   poison oak   cactus

2. pansy   zinnia   petunia   bushes   tulip

3. trunk   eucalyptus   bark   root   branch

4. maple   elm   twig   willow   birch

5. wheat   rice   sugarcane   oats   palm

6. stem   redwood   petal   thorn   bud

A. Which Is It?

► Circle the correct answer.

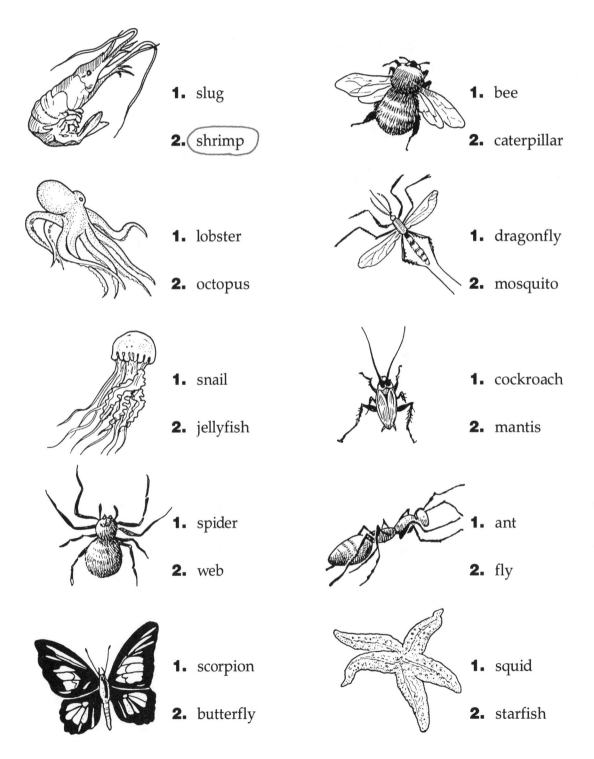

1. slug

2. (shrimp)

1. bee

2. caterpillar

1. lobster

2. octopus

1. dragonfly

2. mosquito

1. snail

2. jellyfish

1. cockroach

2. mantis

1. spider

2. web

1. ant

2. fly

1. scorpion

2. butterfly

1. squid

2. starfish

B. Things With Wings

▶ Write words from exercise A.

Things With Wings

1. _____

2. _____

3. _____

4. _____

5. _____

Things Without Wings

1. _____

2. _____

3. _____

4. _____

5. _____

C. Doubles

▶ Write all the words with double letters.

beetle	scorpion	jellyfish	scallop	mussel	cocoon
web	butterfly	grasshopper	caterpillar	bee	shell

	Word	Double Letters		Word	Double Letters
1.	_____	_____	6.	_____	_____
2.	_____	_____	7.	_____	_____
3.	_____	_____	8.	_____	_____
4.	_____	_____	9.	_____	_____
5.	_____	_____	10.	_____	_____

A. What Is It?

► Look at the picture.

► Write the word.

duck	rattlesnake	swan	shark	turkey
frog	robin		turtle	eagle

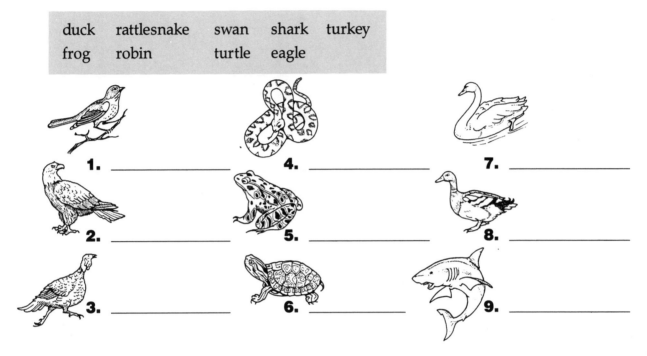

1. _____

2. _____

3. _____

4. _____

5. _____

6. _____

7. _____

8. _____

9. _____

B. Matching

► Match **Animal** and **Category**.

► Write **a**, **b**, or **c** in the blank.

Animal

Category

1. ___ owl

6. ___ crow

a. fish

2. ___ trout

7. ___ flamingo

b. reptile

3. ___ goose

8. ___ cobra

c. bird

4. ___ lizard

9. ___ stingray

5. ___ alligator

10. ___ rooster

C. What Could You See in the Sea?

► Look at the picture.
► Write a bird, fish, or reptile for each place.
► Write the sentence.

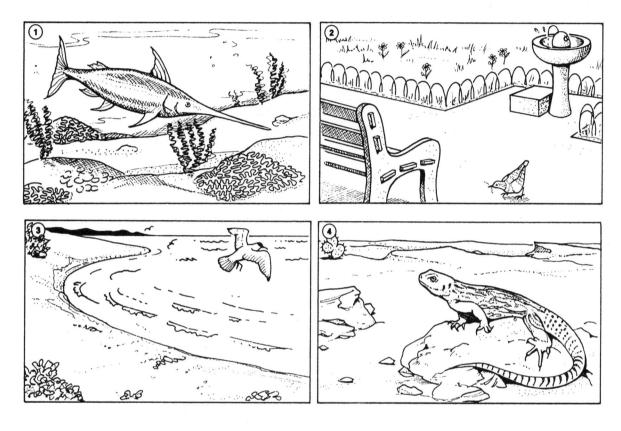

1. I could see a _____ in the sea.

_____

2. I could see a _____ in the park.

_____

3. I could see a _____ in the air.

_____

4. I could see an _____ in the desert.

_____

A. What Is It?

► Look at the picture.
► Write the word.

hippopotamus	dolphin	panda	whale	bear
kangaroo	giraffe	camel	lion	fox

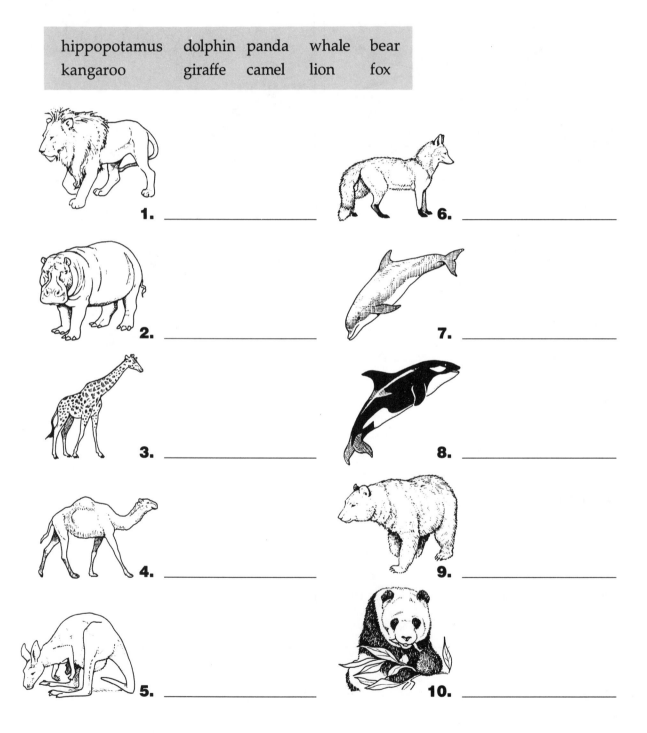

1. _____

2. _____

3. _____

4. _____

5. _____

6. _____

7. _____

8. _____

9. _____

10. _____

B. What's the Word?

▶ Review the words on Dictionary pages **62–65**.

▶ Look at the picture.

▶ Fill in the blanks.

▶ Use some of the letters to write the name of another animal.

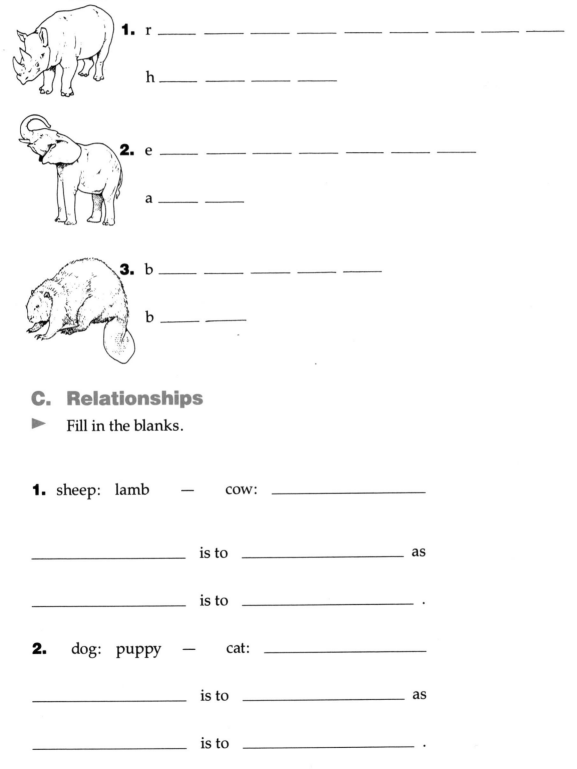

1. r ___ ___ ___ ___ ___ ___ ___ ___ ___

h ___ ___ ___ ___

2. e ___ ___ ___ ___ ___ ___ ___ ___

a ___ ___

3. b ___ ___ ___ ___ ___

b ___ ___

C. Relationships

▶ Fill in the blanks.

1. sheep: lamb — cow: _____

_____ is to _____ as

_____ is to _____ .

2. dog: puppy — cat: _____

_____ is to _____ as

_____ is to _____ .

D. What Goes Together?

► Review the words on Dictionary pages **62–65**.

► Find the words to go in each category.

► Write the words in the blanks.

Animals That Fly:

1. _____   3. _____

2. _____   4. _____

Animals That Jump:

1. _____   3. _____

2. _____   4. _____

Animals That Swim:

1. _____   3. _____

2. _____   4. _____

Animals That Crawl:

1. _____   3. _____

2. _____   4. _____

E. Adopt an Animal

► Look at the pictures on Dictionary pages 66–67.

► Choose an animal to adopt. Tell why you want this animal.

_____

_____

F. Bingo Bongo

▶ Review the words on Dictionary pages **60–69**.

▶ Look for the same words on both the bingo card and the list.

▶ Circle the word on the list.

▶ Cross out the same word on the card.

▶ Cross out five words in a row to win.*

eucalyptus	starfish	hummingbird	porcupine	chimpanzee
lily	scallop	pelican	gopher	walrus
willow	scorpion	duck	donkey	raccoon
orchid	worm	stork	moose	whale
holly	centipede	eel	llama	leopard
rice	squid	parakeet	chipmunk	hyena
palm	grasshopper	rattlesnake	goat	puppy
oak	ladybug	iguana	squirrel	tiger

BINGO CARD				
corn	turkey	baboon	pony	worm
cow	panda	mussel	parakeet	zebra
wasp	bison	tiger	daisy	robin
pheasant	lily	beetle	armadillo	flounder
goat	flounder	leaf	seal	fly

*See Lesson 5, page 13 for examples.   89

A. All the Words

► Write the words in alphabetical order.

Mediterranean	Antarctic	Arabian	Africa	Rocky	Urals	Asia
Antarctica	Caucasus	Indian	Amazon	Andes	Nile	Gobi
Australia	Yangtze	Sahara	Arctic	Congo	Alps	

Words beginning with **A**:

1. _____   6. _____

2. _____   7. _____

3. _____   8. _____

4. _____   9. _____

5. _____   10. _____

All the other words:

1. _____   6. _____

2. _____   7. _____

3. _____   8. _____

4. _____   9. _____

5. _____   10. _____

B. What Doesn't Belong?

► Cross out the word that doesn't belong.

Continents	Asia	Africa	Australia	~~Congo~~
Oceans	Arctic	Pacific	Alps	Atlantic
Seas, Bays, and Gulfs	Painted	Hudson	Red	Black
Mountain Ranges	Rocky	Himalayas	Nile	Appalachian
Deserts	Indian	Sahara	Gobi	Mojave
Rivers	Mississippi	Andes	Amazon	Rio Grande

C. Matching

► Match **Place** and **Description**.

► Write a different letter in each blank.

Place

1. ____ Urals

2. ____ Yangtze

3. ____ Hudson

4. ____ Caribbean

5. ____ Europe

6. ____ Atacama

7. ____ Mexico

8. ____ Antarctic

Description

a. river

b. continent

c. mountain range

d. ocean

e. bay

f. desert

g. gulf

h. sea

D. The Great Explorer

▶ Look at the map and the route from Chile to Florida.

▶ Imagine you are going to take this trip.

▶ Answer the questions with complete sentences.

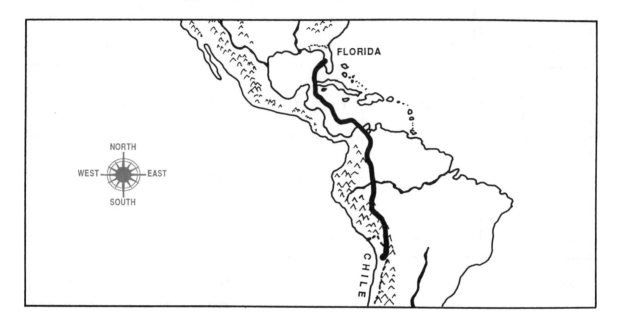

1. Is South America a sea, a gulf, or a continent?

_____

2. What great South American river will you cross?

_____

3. What mountain range will you go over?

_____

4. What sea will you cross in a boat?

_____

5. What other continent will you visit?

_____

53 The United States of America pages 72–73

A. What's the State?

▶ Fill in the blanks.

▶ You can use a word more than once.

▶ Write the sentence.

| Oklahoma | Kentucky | Wyoming | east | west | north | south |

1. The state of _____ is north of Texas, _____ of

Arkansas, south of Kansas, and _____ of New Mexico.

_____

_____

2. The state of _____ is east of Idaho, _____ of Montana,

west of South Dakota and Nebraska, and _____ of Colorado.

_____

_____

3. The state of _____ is south of Ohio and Indiana, _____

of West Virginia, north of Tennessee, and _____ of Illinois

and Missouri.

_____

_____

B. Name the States

1. Name the states on the Atlantic Coast.

_____

2. Name the states on the Pacific Coast.

_____

3. Name the states on the Gulf of Mexico.

_____

4. Name the states north of Texas.

_____

5. Name the states south of Minnesota.

_____

6. Name the state you are living in now.

_____

C. What's Missing?
► Fill in the blank.
► Write the word.

1. H a w a i ____ _____

2. C o n n e ____ t i c u t _____

3. M i s s i s ____ i p p i _____

4. M a s s ____ c h u s e t t s _____

5. P e n n s ____ l v a n i a _____

D. The Great Traveler

▶ Look at the map and the routes from San Francisco to Washington, D.C.

▶ Plan a bicycle trip from east to west or west to east.

▶ Write the states you must pass through, beginning with California or Virginia.

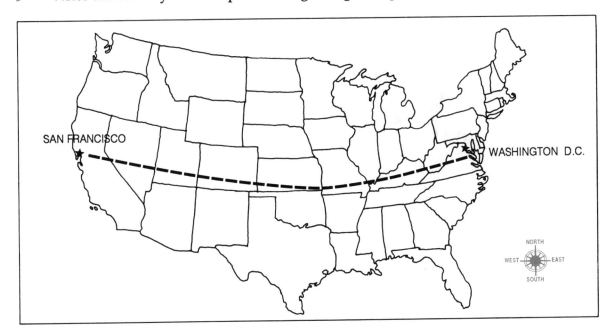

_____

_____

E. Which State?

1. Which state borders the greatest number of other states? _____

How many states does it border? _____

2. Name the states: _____

54 The Universe page 74

A. What's in the Universe?

► Fill in the blanks.

eclipse   orbit   galaxy   Sun   planets

1. The _____ is a very large, hot star.

2. The Earth and the Sun are part of one _____ in the universe.

3. The Earth travels around the Sun in a path, or _____ .

4. When the Moon is between the Earth and the Sun, there is an

_____ .

5. Earth, Mercury, Venus, Mars, Jupiter, and Saturn are _____ .

B. Scrambled Sentences

► Form a sentence with the words.

1. falls   sky   across   comet   A   the

_____

2. is   of   A   group   constellation   stars   many   a

_____

3. see   telescope   We   can   the   stars   through   a

_____

A. What Is It?

▶ Look at the picture.

▶ Write the words.

| astronaut | launchpad | rocket | space suit |

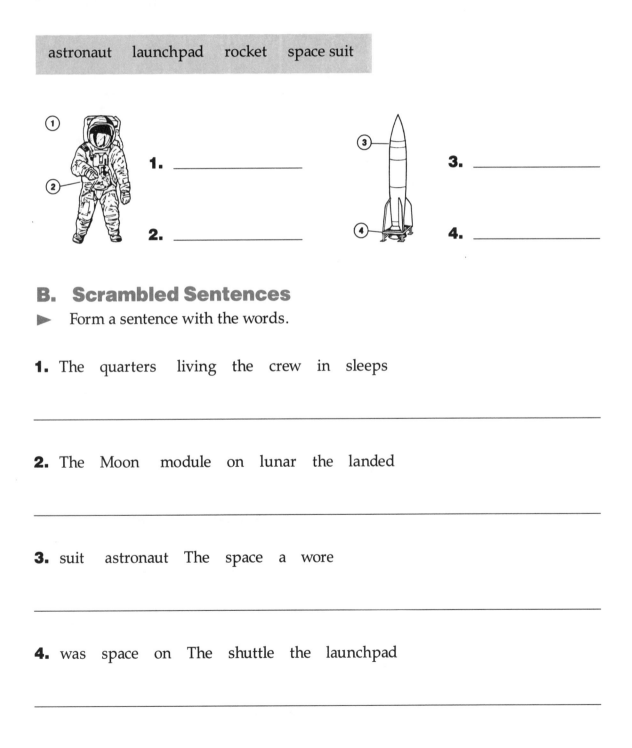

1. _____

2. _____

3. _____

4. _____

B. Scrambled Sentences

▶ Form a sentence with the words.

1. The   quarters   living   the   crew   in   sleeps

_____

2. The   Moon   module   on   lunar   the   landed

_____

3. suit   astronaut   The   space   a   wore

_____

4. was   space   on   The   shuttle   the   launchpad

_____

56 A Classroom page 76

A. What's Different?

► Fill in the blanks.

► Circle the word ending in a different letter.

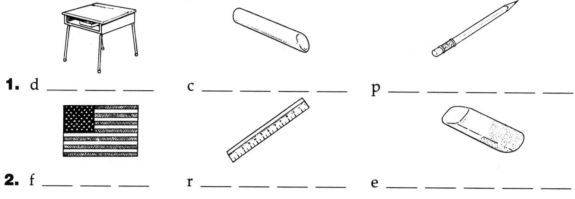

1. d __ __ __   c __ __ __ __   p __ __ __ __ __ __

2. f __ __ __   r __ __ __ __ __   e __ __ __ __ __ __

B. Word Endings

► Look at the words on page 76.

► Write all the words that end in **-r**.

ruler,

_____

C. Can I Write With It?

► Choose words to fit in the appropriate categories.

Things to Write With   **Things to Write In or On**

1. _____   **1.** _____

2. _____   **2.** _____

3. _____   **3.** _____

4. _____   **4.** _____

School Verbs page 77

A. What's the Verb?

▶ Write the verb.

| read | listen | write | type | close | walk |

1. _____

2. _____

3. _____

4. _____

5. _____

6. _____

B. What's Happening?

▶ Look at the picture on Dictionary page 76.

▶ Use verbs from Dictionary page 77 to complete the sentences.

1. The teacher is _____

2. A girl is _____

3. Another girl is _____

4. One boy is _____

5. Another boy is _____

A. Which Is It?

► Circle the correct answer.

► Write the word.

1. scale

2. bench

_____

1. flask

2. petri dish

_____

1. beaker

2. flame

_____

1. magnifying glass

2. safety glasses

_____

1. test tube

2. rubber tubing

_____

1. slide

2. prism

_____

1. Bunsen burner

2. medicine dropper

_____

1. magnet

2. microscope

_____

1. tongs

2. tweezers

_____

B. Things That Hold Water

▶ Write words from exercise A.

Things That Hold Water

Things That Don't Hold Water

1. _____

1. _____

2. _____

2. _____

3. _____

3. _____

4. _____

4. _____

C. What Do You Use?

▶ Look at the picture in the Dictionary.

▶ Answer in complete sentences.

1. What could you sit on in a lab?

_____

2. What could you use to see with?

_____

3. What could you use to hold a test tube?

_____

4. What could you use to pour water into a test tube?

_____

5. What could you use to boil water?

_____

A. You're the Artist

▶ Fill in the blanks.

▶ Draw lines and shapes.

▶ Write the words.

1. t r i a n g l e △ _____

2. s __ __ __ __ __   _____

3. r __ __ __ __   a __ __ __ __   _____

4. p __ __ __ __ __ __ __

   l __ __ __ __   _____

5. c __ __ __ __ __ __   _____

B. How Big Is It?

▶ Look at the picture.

▶ Fill in the blanks.

| height | depth | width |

1. The _____ of the bookcase is 30 inches.

2. The _____ of the bookcase is 18 inches.

3. The _____ of the bookcase is 15 inches.

C. A Crossword Puzzle

► Look at the pictures.
► Complete the words.

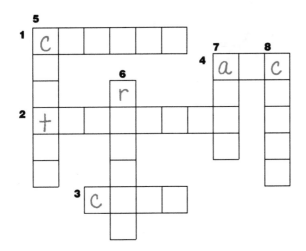

Across:

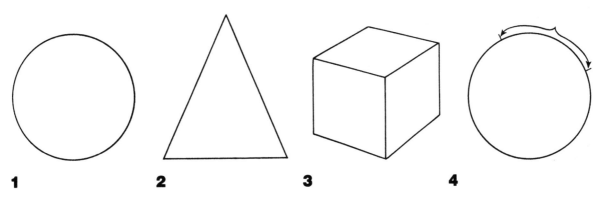

1   2   3   4

Down:

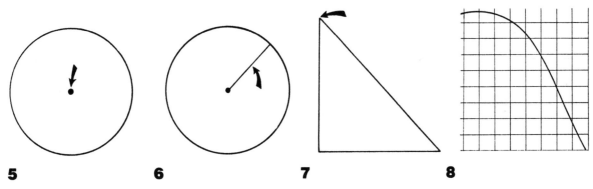

5   6   7   8

A. What Is It?

► Look at the picture.
► Write the word.

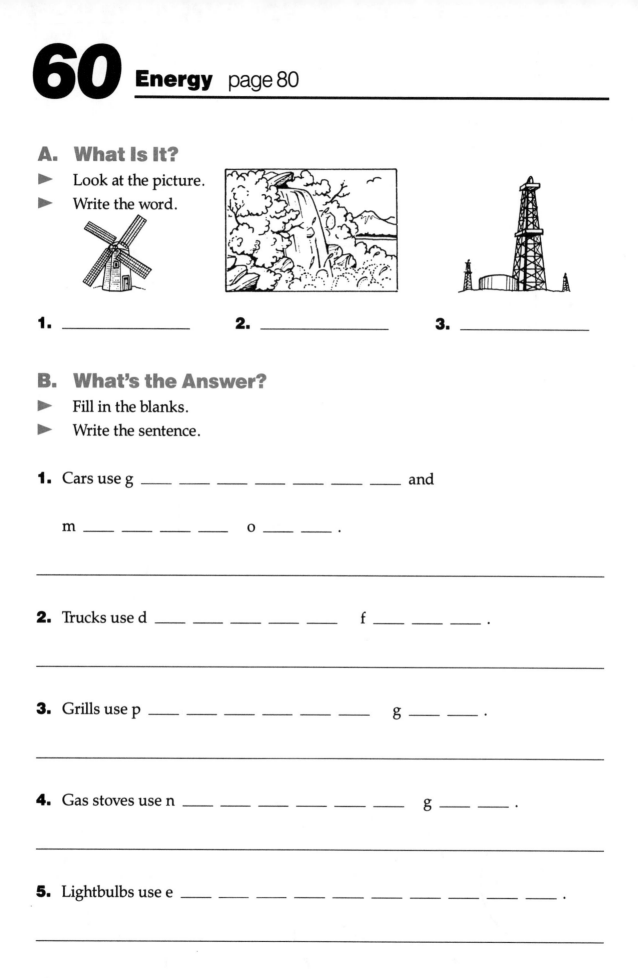

1. _____   **2.** _____   **3.** _____

B. What's the Answer?

► Fill in the blanks.
► Write the sentence.

1. Cars use g ___ ___ ___ ___ ___ ___ ___ and

m ___ ___ ___ ___ o ___ ___ .

_____

2. Trucks use d ___ ___ ___ ___ ___   f ___ ___ ___ .

_____

3. Grills use p ___ ___ ___ ___ ___ ___   g ___ ___ .

_____

4. Gas stoves use n ___ ___ ___ ___ ___ ___   g ___ ___ .

_____

5. Lightbulbs use e ___ ___ ___ ___ ___ ___ ___ ___ .

_____

61 Farming and Ranching page 81

A. What Do You See?

► Look at the picture.
► Write the words.

barn	fence	silo	fruit tree	dairy cow
farmhouse	farmer	field	orchard	pitchfork

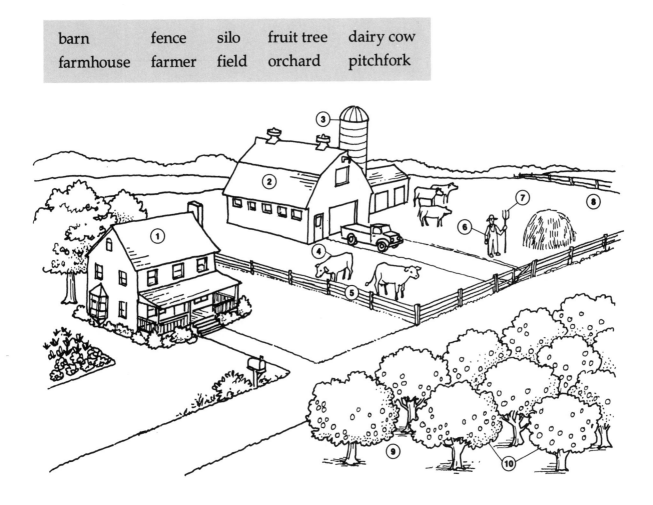

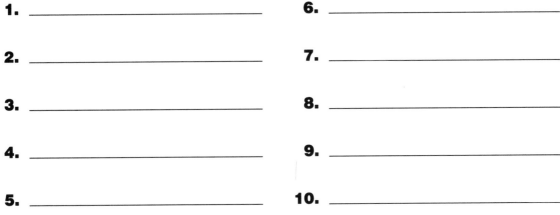

1. _____   6. _____

2. _____   7. _____

3. _____   8. _____

4. _____   9. _____

5. _____   10. _____

B. How Many Words?

► Write all the new words you can.
► Check spelling in a larger dictionary.

1. livestock

_____ _____ _____ _____

_____ _____ _____ _____

2. scarecrow

_____ _____ _____ _____

_____ _____ _____ _____

C. What Doesn't Belong?

► Cross out the word that doesn't belong.

Buildings	farmhouse	trough	silo	barn
People	scarecrow	farmer	cowboy	cowgirl
Animals	sheep	horses	cattle	orchard
Tools	tractor	combine	livestock	pitchfork

A. What Is It?

▶ Look at the picture.
▶ Write the word.

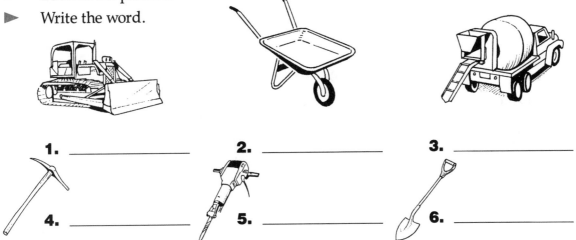

1. _____   **2.** _____   **3.** _____

4. _____   **5.** _____   **6.** _____

B. Word Circles

▶ Circle the words that go together.

1. pickax   shovel   level   rung

2. foundation   builder   construction worker   linesman

3. board   level   bricks   cement

4. cement mixer   backhoe   blueprints   jackhammer

C. What Do You Say?

▶ Choose words to fit in the appropriate categories.

1. Parts of a building: _____

2. Workers: _____

3. Tools/Equipment: _____

63 An Office page 83

A. What Is It?
► Look at the picture.
► Write the word.

| calendar | photocopier | telephone |
| computer | typewriter | file cabinet |

1. _____

2. _____

3. _____

4. _____

5. _____

6. _____

B. What's the Answer?
► Look at the picture in the Dictionary.
► Fill in the blanks.

1. The t ___ ___ ___ ___ ___ is reading a

p ___ ___ ___ ___ ___ ___ ___ .

2. The s ___ ___ ___ ___ ___ ___ ___ ___ ___

o ___ ___ ___ ___ ___ ___ ___ is answering the phone.

3. The m ___ ___ ___ ___ ___ ___ is using a

c ___ ___ ___ ___ ___ ___ ___ ___ ___ .

4. The f ___ ___ ___   c ___ ___ ___ ___ is looking for a file

f ___ ___ ___ ___ ___ .

108

A. What Do You Say?

▶ Fill in the blanks with an appropriate response.

Family　　　　　　　　　　　　　　　　**Occupation**

1. Father:　　　　　　　　　　　　　　　He's a _____

2. Mother:　　　　　　　　　　　　　　She's a _____

3. Brother:　　　　　　　　　　　　　　_____

4. Sister:　　　　　　　　　　　　　　　_____

5. Husband/Wife:　　　　　　　　　　_____

6. Son/Daughter:　　　　　　　　　　_____

7. My occupation:　　　　　　　　　　_____

8. Occupation I would like:　　　　　_____

B. Would a Carpenter Work With Wood?

▶ Look at the pictures on Dictionary page 85.
▶ Fill in the blanks.

1. A _carpenter_ works with wood.

2. A _____ fixes pipes.

3. An _____ makes outlets for plugs.

4. A _____ dusts furniture.

5. A _____ supervises shop workers.

109

C. Where Do They Work?

► Review the words on Dictionary pages 102-103.

► Look at the picture on Dictionary page 84.

► Write **a**, **b**, or **c** in the blank.

1. _____ The florist works next to the

   a. jeweller.   b. baker.   c. optician.

2. _____ The pharmacist works across from the

   a. baker.   b. butcher.   c. repairperson.

3. _____ The tailor works to the left of the

   a. barber.   b. greengrocer.   c. hairdresser.

4. _____ The travel agent works between the barber and the

   a. mechanic.   b. repairperson.   c. optician.

5. _____ The mechanic works between the barber and the

   a. florist.   b. optician.   c. pharmacist.

6. _____ The baker works next to the

   a. optician.   b. mechanic.   c. butcher.

7. _____ The repairperson works between the travel agent and the

   a. pharmacist.   b. jeweller.   c. tailor.

D. What's the Answer?

► Fill in the blanks.

► Write the sentence.

1. A m <u>e</u> <u>s</u> <u>s</u> <u>e</u> <u>n</u> <u>g</u> <u>e</u> <u>r</u> carries messages.

   <u>A messenger carries messages.</u>

2. An a ___ ___ ___ ___ ___ paints pictures.

   _____

3. An a ___ ___ ___ ___ ___ ___ ___ ___ designs buildings.

   _____

4. A t ___ ___ ___ ___ ___ sews clothes.

   _____

5. A d ___ ___ ___ j ___ ___ ___ ___ ___ plays records.

   _____

6. A p ___ ___ ___ ___ ___ ___ ___ ___ ___ ___ takes

   photographs.

   _____

7. A h ___ ___ ___ ___ ___ ___ ___ ___ ___ styles hair.

   _____

A. What's the Answer?

► Look at the picture in the Dictionary.
► Fill in the blanks.
► Write the sentence.

1. Many children are playing on the

p ___ ___ ___ ___ ___ ___ ___ ___ ___ .

_____

2. There is a h ___ ___ ___ ___ ___ ___ ___ ___

r ___ ___ ___ ___ on the b ___ ___ ___ ___ ___ path.

_____

3. Children are playing on the s ___ ___ ___ ___ ___ .

_____

4. There are joggers on the j ___ ___ ___ ___ ___ ___ p ___ ___ ___ .

_____

B. Where's the Band? Where's the Sand?

► Write a place for each item.

1. the band _band shell_

2. the sand _____

3. water _____

4. wild animals _____

5. trash _____

6. ducks _____

66 Outdoor Activities pages 88–89

A. What's the Answer?

► Look at the picture in the Dictionary.

► Fill in the blanks.

► Write the sentence.

| park ranger   fishing rod   camp stove   raft |

1. The fisherman is putting bait on the hook of her

f ___ ___ ___ ___ ___ ___   r ___ ___.

_____

_____

2. The riders in the r ___ ___ ___ are wearing life vests.

_____

3. The p ___ ___ ___   r ___ ___ ___ ___ ___ is riding a horse.

_____

4. The man by the c ___ ___ ___   s ___ ___ ___ ___ is holding a

coffee pot.

_____

B. Matching

► Match **People** and **Place**.

► Write a different letter in each blank.

	People		Place
1.	_d_ the campers	**a.**	at the picnic table
2.	___ the fishermen	**b.**	on the mountain
3.	___ the family	**c.**	in the stream
4.	___ the rafters	**d.**	in the woods
5.	___ the climbers	**e.**	in the river

C. I Know Where the Campers Are!

► Write questions and answers with the words in exercise B.

1. Question: _Where are the campers?_

Answer: _The campers are in the woods._

2. Question: _____

Answer: _____

3. Question: _____

Answer: _____

4. Question: _____

Answer: _____

5. Question: _____

Answer: _____

67 At the Beach pages 90–91

A. What Do You See?

▶ Look at the picture.

▶ Write the words.

shovel	bathing trunks	beach umbrella	cooler	beach chair
towel	bathing suit	suntan lotion	pail	sunglasses

1. _____

2. _____

3. _____

4. _____

5. _____

6. _____

7. _____

8. _____

9. _____

10. _____

B. Word Circles

▶ Circle the words that go together.

1. snorkel   wet suit   scuba tank   flippers   shell

2. bathing suit   bathing trunks   bathing towel   lifeboat

3. beach ball   kite   pail   shovel   motel

4. life preserver   whistle   lifeguard   sandcastle

5. sunglasses   suntan lotion   beach umbrella   refreshment stand

C. What Are They Doing?

▶ Look at the picture in the Dictionary.
▶ Write **a**, **b**, or **c** in the blank.

1. _____ A boy is surfing on

    a. a towel.   b. a surfboard.   c. an air mattress.

2. _____ The lifeguard is looking through

    a. binoculars.   b. dunes.   c. a cooler.

3. _____ A sunbather is putting on

    a. a whistle.   b. a wet suit.   c. suntan lotion.

4. _____ The runners are running on the

    a. boardwalk.   b. waves.   c. sand.

5. _____ A swimmer is swimming in the

    a. lifeboat.   b. motel.   c. water.

68 Team Sports page 92
Ballfields page 93

A. All the Words

▶ Write the words in alphabetical order.

hockey stick	halfback	uniform	pitcher
home plate	baseball	catcher's mitt	coach
goal	scoreboard	split end	center fielder
cheerleader	helmet	stands	shortstop

Words beginning with **c**:   Words beginning with **s**:   Words beginning with **h**:

1. _____   1. _____   1. _____

2. _____   2. _____   2. _____

3. _____   3. _____   3. _____

4. _____   4. _____   4. _____

B. What Doesn't Belong?

▶ Cross out the word that doesn't belong.

People	umpire	shortstop	referee	puck
Place	cap	diamond	field	dugout
Equipment	glove	bat	guard	stick
Sport	volleyball	lacrosse	soccer	fullback

117

C. Where's the Fun?

▶ Review the words on Dictionary page 103.
▶ Underline the correct answers.
▶ Write the sentence.

1. At the softball game, the (pitcher, catcher, umpire) is throwing the ball

(at, for, to) the batter.

_____

_____

2. At the baseball game, the (pitcher, catcher, batter) is going to hit the ball

(over, under, through) the fence.

_____

_____

3. At the football game, the (referee, quarterback, coach) is passing the ball

(on, away from, across) the field.

_____

_____

4. The (volleyball, basketball, soccer) player is jumping high to put the ball

(over, under, in) the net.

_____

_____

A. What Do You Say?

► Fill in the blanks.

tennis	bowling	boxing	horse racing
Ping-Pong	golf	gymnastics	handball
racquetball	ice skating	skiing	track and field

1. Indoor sports:

_____   _____

_____   _____

2. Outdoor sports:

_____   _____

_____   _____

3. Sports I like to watch:

_____   _____

_____   _____

4. Sports I like to play:

_____   _____

_____   _____

B. What Doesn't Belong?

▶ Cross out the word that doesn't belong.

People	runner	jockey	gymnast	racket
Place	track	putter	green	lane
Equipment	pin	saddle	boxer	paddle
Sport	gymnastics	gutter	handball	tennis

C. Where's the Ball? Where's the Player?

▶ Look at the pictures in the Dictionary.
▶ Complete the sentences.

1. You play tennis on a _____

2. You play golf on a _____

3. You play Ping-Pong on a _____

4. You run on a _____

5. You skate on a _____

6. You ski on a _____

7. You box in a _____

A. What's the Verb?

▶ Write the verb.

hit	dive	kick	fall	ride
throw	catch	jump	skate	run

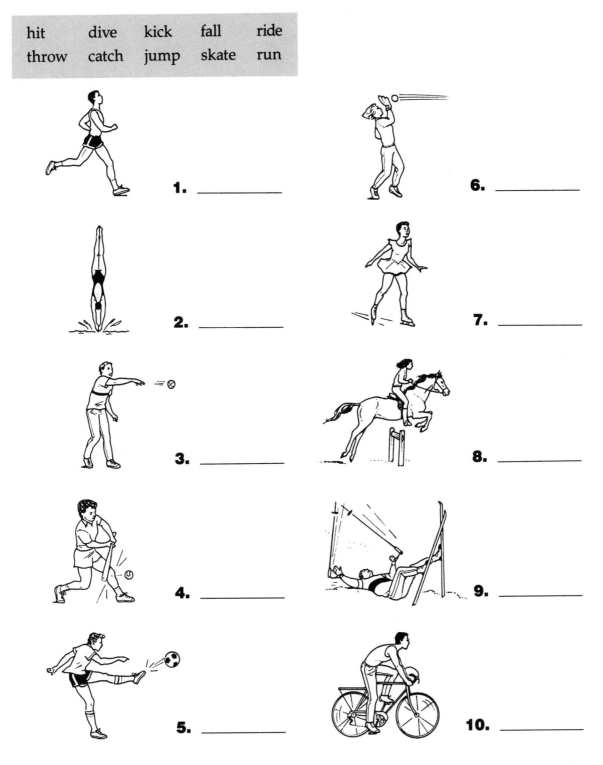

1. _____

2. _____

3. _____

4. _____

5. _____

6. _____

7. _____

8. _____

9. _____

10. _____

B. Matching

► Match **Sport** and **Sports Verb**.

► Write **a**, **b**, **c**, **d**, **e**, **f**, or **g** in the blanks.

► There may be more than one correct answer.

Sport	Sports Verb
1. _____ ice hockey	**a.** hit
2. _____ baseball	**b.** jump
3. _____ volleyball	**c.** serve
4. _____ basketball	**d.** skate
5. _____ soccer	**e.** kick
6. _____ ice skating	**f.** catch
7. _____ golf	**g.** run
8. _____ football	

71 **Musical Instruments** page 98

A. What Is It?

▶ Look at the picture.

▶ Write the word.

| violin | drum | guitar | piano | trumpet | flute |

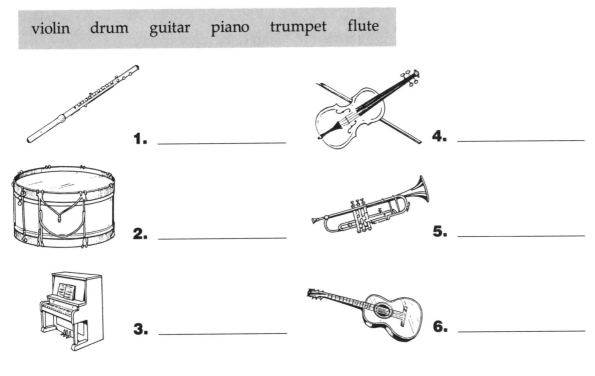

1. _____

2. _____

3. _____

4. _____

5. _____

6. _____

B. Scrambled Sentences

▶ Form a sentence with the words.

1. a   clarinet   than   A   tuba   bigger   is

_____

2. different   are   xylophones   from   Accordians

_____

3. harp   that   yours?   Is

_____

A. What's the Answer?

► Look at the pictures in the Dictionary.
► Fill in the blanks.
► Write the sentence.

1. The u ___ ___ ___ ___ showed the man to his seat with a

f ___ ___ ___ ___ ___ ___ ___ ___ ___.

_____

2. The a ___ ___ ___ ___ ___ ___ ___ watched the

b ___ ___ ___ ___ ___ .

_____

3. The d ___ ___ ___ ___ ___ ___ danced on the s ___ ___ ___ ___ .

_____

4. The conductor on the p ___ ___ ___ ___ ___ led the orchestra with a

b ___ ___ ___ ___ .

_____

5. The c ___ ___ ___ ___ ___ sang a song.

_____

B. Who's on Stage?

► Review the words on Dictionary page 102.
► Look at the picture of the Rock Group in the Dictionary.
► Underline the correct answer.

1. The singer is between the bass guitarist and the

   a. drummer.
   b. keyboard player.
   c. lead guitarist.

2. The drummer is behind the

   a. singer.
   b. keyboard player.
   c. lead guitarist.

3. The lead guitarist is playing the

   a. drums.
   b. electric guitar.
   c. synthesizer.

4. The keyboard player is next to the

   a. bass guitarist.
   b. singer.
   c. lead guitarist.

5. The drummer is playing the

   a. drums.
   b. synthesizer.
   c. electric guitar.

A. What Is It?

▶ Look at the picture.

▶ Write the word.

| turntable | camera | slide projector | VCR | screen | headphones |

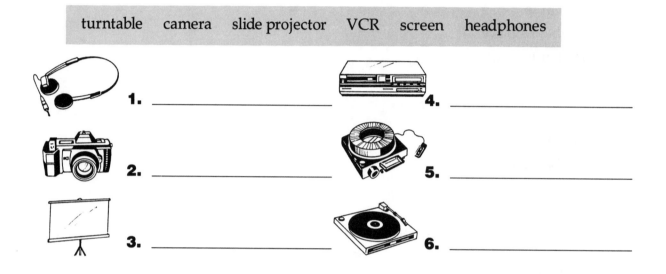

1. _____

2. _____

3. _____

4. _____

5. _____

6. _____

B. Things You Listen To

▶ Look at the pictures in the Dictionary.

▶ Choose words to fit in the appropriate categories.

Things You Listen To

1. _____

2. _____

3. _____

4. _____

Things You Watch

1. _____

2. _____

3. _____

4. _____

A. Matching

▶ Match the items that go together.

▶ Write a different letter in each blank.

1. ____ button   **a.** pincushion

2. ____ hem   **b.** eye

3. ____ hook   **c.** pattern

4. ____ pin   **d.** buttonhole

5. ____ pattern piece   **e.** hem binding

B. What's the Answer?

▶ Fill in the blanks.

▶ Write the sentence.

1. You cut m ___ ___ ___ ___ ___ ___ ___ with

   s ___ ___ ___ ___ ___ ___ ___ .

   _____

2. You measure with a t ___ ___ ___   m ___ ___ ___ ___ ___ ___ .

   _____

3. You can sew a blouse on a s ___ ___ ___ ___ ___

   m ___ ___ ___ ___ ___ ___ .

   _____

75 Prepositions of Description page 102*

A. Where's the Cat?
▶ Look at the picture in the Dictionary.
▶ Underline the correct answer.
▶ Write the sentence.

1. The cat is (on, under) the rug.

_____

2. The cat is (on, next to) the TV.

_____

3. The cat is (in front of, behind) the chair.

_____

4. The cat is (in, at) the drawer.

_____

5. The cat is (in front of, above) the fireplace.

_____

B. Where Are You?
▶ Answer in complete sentences.

1. Where are you sitting right now? _____

2. Who or what are you next to? _____

3. Who or what is in front of you? _____

*See also Lesson 19.

A. Where's the Golf Ball?

► Look at the picture in the Dictionary.
► Underline the correct answer.
► Write the sentence.

1. The ball is going (down, into) the hill.

_____

2. The ball is going (from, across) the water.

_____

3. The ball is going (around, over) the lighthouse.

_____

4. The ball is going (away from, over) the bridge.

_____

5. The ball is going (toward, up) the hole.

_____

6. The couple is going (to, through) the golf course.

_____

7. The family is coming (up, from) the golf course.

_____

*See also Lesson 35.

B. Follow That Dog!

► Look at the picture.
► What did Spot do?

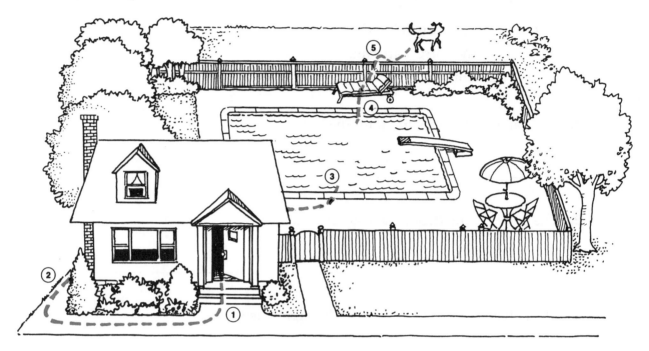

Spot went:

1. _____ the house.

2. _____ the house.

3. _____ the pool.

4. _____ the pool.

5. _____ the fence.